the *natural* menopause cookbook

the *natural* menopause cookbook

Ease your symptoms with over 70 delicious recipes

Angie Jefferson and Fiona Hunter

hamlyn

First published in Great Britain in 2004 by
Hamlyn, a division of Octopus Publishing Group Ltd
2–4 Heron Quays, London E14 4JP

ISBN 0 600 60923 5

A CIP catalogue record for this book is available from the British Library

Printed in China

10 9 8 7 6 5 4 3 2 1

While this book provides information on the menopause and an approach to managing the symptoms by diet, it is not medical advice and is not intended to be a substitute for a thorough assessment of your condition by your doctor or medical practitioner.

contents

introduction

About this book

The menopause can be a time of confusion and mixed emotions. Unsure of what is happening to our bodies, and bombarded with conflicting stories about hormone replacement therapy (HRT), most of us find it difficult to get practical and accurate information. This book provides a simple and down-to-earth approach to the menopause years and offers advice on how to take control of any troublesome symptoms before they take control of you. In the following pages you will find the information you need to manage the symptoms and effects of the menopause, both today and in the years to come.

The menopause is a natural part of a woman's life, signalling an end to her fertile years. While some women sail through it with little difficulty, others experience a range of symptoms which vary in severity from mild to completely disrupting. Over the past decade HRT has increased in popularity and is used successfully by many, both to treat symptoms and provide health benefits. However, there are health concerns regarding HRT – some women cannot use it and others simply would rather not. But HRT is not the only approach available; changing your diet can offer an effective, alternative management strategy.

This book has been written for all menopausal women, whatever their symptoms, and whether or not they are taking HRT. It does not matter whether you are just entering the menopause or have been experiencing its effects for some time. The information here will allow you to get the best you can from what you eat, and help alleviate common symptoms.

First we review the changes that are happening to you, and common symptoms and effects arising from these. We then look at healthy eating during the menopause, managing your weight and specific areas of the diet from which you can gain the most benefit. The main section of the book brings your new diet to life with a wide range of tasty and enjoyable recipes.

As with any new diet, the body may require some time to adjust to the changes that you are making and you may not appreciate the full benefits for several months. Be patient and persevere – the boost to your overall health will help you get through the menopause with ease.

What is the menopause?

The menopause is defined by those in the medical profession as the final menstrual period, and signals the end of a woman's fertility. However, the term is more commonly used to describe the time leading up to the final menstrual period and the time beyond.

For most women, the start of the menopause is signalled by their periods becoming increasingly irregular, until they eventually stop. The menopause is considered to be over when no periods have occurred for a year.

The average age that women go through this change is 51 years, but it can occur at any time between the ages of 45 and 55. It is considered premature if it occurs before the age of 40, something which is thought to affect 1 in 100 women. It may also be suddenly induced at any age as a result of illness or a medical procedure, such as a hysterectomy where the ovaries are removed.

What causes it?

The menopause occurs when your ovaries simply run out of the eggs they release each month during your fertile years. Before puberty the ovaries are packed with eggs and during a woman's life around 450 of them mature and are released to travel down the fallopian tubes and into the womb. This is ovulation. If the egg does not become fertilized, it will pass out of the body along with the womb lining (menstruation). The menstrual cycle is under the control of hormones, and these cause an egg to be released each month and prepare the body for possible fertilization. One of the main hormones is oestrogen, which is produced by the ovaries themselves.

Around the age of 45, few eggs remain and the ovaries start to reduce their production of the hormone oestrogen, until it stops altogether during the menopausal years. During this time the female body has to adapt from a life that has been dominated by oestrogen and the menstrual cycle, to a life without this hormone. It is this decline in oestrogen that results in the symptoms many women suffer.

Menopause: ceasing of menstruation; period in a woman's life when this occurs.
– Oxford English Dictionary

above Changing diet can help to manage the menopause.

How do women react?

How women experience the menopause depends on several factors, including their diet and nutrition, their general fitness and physical health, and may even be influenced by women's beliefs and attitudes towards the menopause.

What are the symptoms?

Early physical symptoms	Emotional symptoms	Later physical symptoms
Hot flushes	Mood swings and irritability	Dry skin
Night sweats	Inability to cope	Vaginal dryness
Headaches	Lowered self-esteem	Frequent and/or painful urination
Tiredness	Loss of concentration and short-	Stress or urge incontinence
Insomnia	term memory	Loss of libido
General aches	Anxiety and depression	Painful sexual intercourse

Menopausal symptoms can last for just a few months or linger for several years. It is estimated that three-quarters of Western women experience one or more of the common symptoms associated with the menopause, and that for one-third of those women the symptoms are severe.

Commonly used terms
- Premenopausal – usually a woman in her mid forties who is on the cusp of the menopause.
- Perimenopausal – a woman who is in the midst of the menopause.
- Postmenopausal – a woman who has been period-free for at least a year.

Long-term effects of the menopause

In the long term, the changing oestrogen levels in the body have far-reaching effects on the bones, heart and blood vessels. Oestrogen has a protective effect over the heart, arteries and veins, and helps promote bone density.

As oestrogen levels decline, the risk of developing osteoporosis or heart disease increases significantly. By the age of 50, one in three women are affected by osteoporosis, and almost one-third of premature deaths in women are due to heart disease.

Hormone Replacement Therapy (HRT)

HRT can help alleviate the symptoms of the menopause. As the name suggests, it replaces the hormones that are no longer produced by the body – this includes both oestrogen and another hormone, progesterone. There are many different combinations and strengths of HRT, and different modes of delivery, including tablets, patches, gels and implants. Some continue to give a period every month, others every three months and some no periods at all. Each woman needs to be individually assessed by their doctor to decide which preparation is the right one for them.

below HRT is highly effective, but not the choice of all women.

Pros and cons of HRT

HRT helps to relieve symptoms such as hot flushes, night sweats and vaginal dryness. It may also offer some protection against heart disease, osteoporosis and Alzheimer's, although in order to gain most benefit for these conditions, HRT needs to be taken for at least 5–10 years.

However, as with any drug treatment, HRT also holds some negative effects, which include an increased chance of breast cancer and deep vein thrombosis. As we have already seen, HRT is thought to protect women against heart disease, but recent evidence has suggested that specific types of HRT may actually increase the risk. Current advice by the British Heart Foundation (2003) is that women should not take HRT just to avoid heart problems.

It is important for all women to weigh up the benefits and drawbacks that come with HRT. Make your decision with the help of your doctor to ensure that you are making the best choice for your health.

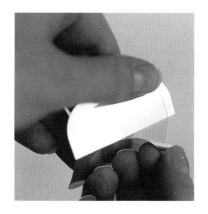

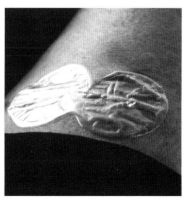

Phytoestrogens – nature's choice

Phytoestrogens are chemicals found in some plants, and are very similar in structure to the human hormone oestrogen. Phytoestrogens appear to promote the effects of oestrogen in some parts of the body. Studies suggest that eating a diet rich in these plant chemicals holds the potential to alleviate some menopausal symptoms, and may also help to prevent the development of breast cancer, osteoporosis and heart disease. A phytoestrogen-rich diet offers benefits for men too, protecting the bones, heart and circulation, and reducing the risk of developing cancer of the prostate. One of the richest sources of phytoestrogens is soya, and foods made from this bean (tofu, soya milk, soya yogurts and so on). They are also found in other beans, linseeds (flax) and rye. How effective they are will depend on how often you eat them, and how much you have.

below Linseed (flax) is a rich source of phytoestrogens and delicious if toasted and sprinkled over cereal or salads.

Compared to HRT, phytoestrogens provide much less oestrogen, but they can help to counteract the fall in levels around the time of the menopause. Phytoestrogens appear to actually reduce the effects of oestrogen in certain parts of the body, however. This is believed to be down to different types of body cell receptors for oestrogen. Oestrogen receptors sit on the outside surfaces of cells and act like lock-and-key mechanisms, allowing the cell to react to oestrogen and phytoestrogens. One specific group of receptors, known as alpha-receptors, occur mainly on the sexual organs such as the uterus, ovaries and breasts, and these respond strongly to oestrogen and weakly to phytoestrogens. The other type, beta-oestrogen receptors, are more common on bones and blood vessels, and these react more strongly to phytoestrogens.

Phytoestrogens in the diet

There are various different types of phytoestrogens, which are found in different foods, and isoflavones are found in the most commonly eaten foods. The average intake of phytoestrogens in a Western diet is estimated to be just 1–2 mg per day. This may be slightly higher among people eating vegetarian diets containing lots of beans and pulses. Women in Japan and other Eastern countries eat 50–100 mg per day, the amount shown by scientists to provide health benefits.

The great news is that foods that are rich in phytoestrogens are all extremely good for us anyway, containing protein, dietary fibre and a wide range of vitamins and minerals. Even if we disregard the potential benefits from phytoestrogens, these foods are all well worth including in a healthy balanced diet.

Phytoestrogens and where to find them

Phytoestrogen type	Where they are found
Isoflavones	Peas, beans, soya beans and soya products, lentils, chickpeas
Coumestans	Sprouting beans, such as clover or alfalfa sprouts
Lignans	Linseeds, rye; small amounts in most other cereals, fruit and vegetables
Prenylated Flavenoids	Hops – some beers

Phytoestrogens and hot flushes

The menopause is much less of a problem in countries where a soya-based diet is eaten, such as Japan and China. In Europe, 80 per cent of menopausal women suffer from hot flushes, compared to 57 per cent in Malaysia and just 18 per cent in China. For one-third of women in Western countries, hot flushes are frequent and severe, and may be accompanied by other symptoms such as headaches, irritability and tiredness. In Japan, hot flushes are so rare that there are no words to describe this experience in the Japanese language.

However, Japanese women still have menopausal symptoms and report an increase in back and neck aches. It may be that a phytoestrogen-rich diet changes the symptoms of the menopause, or that Western women do in fact experience the same symptoms, but are more aware of the problems associated with hot flushes.

The evidence

Most studies have shown that eating phytoestrogen-rich soya over a 2–3 month period can reduce the frequency and severity of hot flushes. In the main, trials have shown a significant impact when 40–80 mg of phytoestrogens are consumed per day. However, there have also been studies where no effects have been found. The greatest benefits will occur if at present you eat little soya, if your hot flushes are severe and if you start to eat at least 45 mg every day.

Soya, cholesterol and heart disease

The death rate from heart disease in Eastern countries, such as Japan and China, is six times lower than death rates in Western countries, such as the UK and the USA. The incidence of heart disease is also lower among vegetarians and vegans than those who eat meat. While many factors are likely to play a part, it is believed that a high intake of soya is one of the factors protecting the heart in Asian and vegetarian diets.

Soya protein, soya fibre and soya phytoestrogens are all known to have a positive influence over the heart, helping to lower the fat content of the diet, lower cholesterol levels, prevent cholesterol being deposited into blood vessel walls and lower blood pressure. If you include soya foods regularly in your diet, you will be gaining all these benefits at once.

below Alfalfa sprouts are a useful source of phytoestrogens and great in salads.

bottom Some traditionally brewed beers contain phytoestrogens.

How much do I need?

Scientific studies have shown that by eating 25 g of soya protein every day you can lower your cholesterol levels by up to 10 per cent. To get 25 g of soya protein, you need to eat around three servings of a soya-based food.

This happens to be the same amount you need to provide 45 mg of phytoestrogens per day – the amount needed to relieve hot flushes. Each of your three servings must provide a minimum of 6.25 g of soya protein, which needs to retain its naturally occurring phytoestrogens (see page 17).

Phytoestrogens and osteoporosis

Osteoporosis is a condition caused by loss of bone mineral, resulting in bones that are weak, fragile and extremely vulnerable to fracture. A range of factors are required to maintain good bone health, one of which is oestrogen. The decline in oestrogen levels during the menopause leads to an increase in the normal rate of mineral loss from bone, and as a result makes postmenopausal women much more vulnerable to osteoporosis.

HRT is known to be effective in preventing osteoporosis, but women consuming diets rich in soya products also have a much-reduced incidence of osteoporosis, suggesting a role for phytoestrogens in preserving bone health.

The evidence

Studies seem to suggest that postmenopausal women who are given phytoestrogen-rich soya have better bone density. The amounts consumed have been in the range of 45–90 mg of phytoestrogens per day, and better effects usually result from higher intakes.

So far, most studies have only lasted six months, whereas any significant improvements in bone structure take around two years. The main benefits have been seen in the spine, which is not surprising as bone 'turnover' here is much quicker than in other parts of the body. It is assumed that, given enough time, beneficial effects would be seen in the hips as well. However, the long-term effects of phytoestrogens on bone health still remain to be explored.

Making claims

Since 2002, manufacturers of soya products in the UK and USA have been able to make a health claim on their packaging that 'including at least 25 g per day of soya protein as part of a diet low in saturated fat can help to reduce blood cholesterol'.

Words of caution about phytoestrogens

It would be naïve to assume that consuming high doses of any substance is always beneficial, and phytoestrogens are no exception. Evidence suggests that the benefits from both phytoestrogens and soya are far greater if they are derived from natural foods (as nature intended and where overdosing is less likely) rather than from concentrated supplements.

One group of women who should exercise caution are those who have breast cancer. Cancerous cells in the breast are generally stimulated by oestrogen, and it is unclear at present as to whether phytoestrogens stimulate or inhibit these cells. Research is underway to answer this question.

Some experts believe that food-derived phytoestrogens do not present a risk to those with breast cancer, but do not recommend phytoestrogen supplements for these women. Other experts believe that phytoestrogens from any source can be damaging to women with breast cancer. Until we have a definite answer it is prudent to be cautious and for those affected not to increase their intake of phytoestrogens, either by diet or supplementation.

A second group who should be aware of the potential effects of a higher phytoestrogen intake are women taking thyroxine. Phytoestrogens may affect thyroxine replacement therapy. If you increase your intake of phytoestrogens you should inform your doctor who will monitor your blood thyroxine levels more closely and adjust your therapy accordingly.

How to eat more phytoestrogens

As we have seen, studies suggest that we need to eat at least 45 mg of phytoestrogens per day to have a beneficial effect. The richest dietary sources include soya beans and foods made from these, lentils, chickpeas, sprouting beans, linseeds, rye, most cereals and fruit and vegetables. Reading this list it may strike you that the richest sources are foods that you never eat, for example soya and linseeds. Don't panic – you don't need to turn into a seed-nibbling vegetarian. There are many simple and easy ways to incorporate these into your daily diet. It is possible to achieve this without lots of home cooking, but the recipes in this book provide great ideas to add interest and variety to your diet.

Imitating nature
A synthetic phytoestrogen (Ipriflavone) is used to treat osteoporosis. The effective dose of this drug is, however, much, much higher than could be achieved by dietary means (200–600 mg per day, compared to the 50–100 mg in a traditional soya-rich Japanese diet).

How much do foods contain?

The phytoestrogen content of foods will vary, and processing may reduce a food's content. Many foods with phytoestrogen-rich ingredients, such as soya or linseeds, do not provide information on the label with the actual phytoestrogen content. Rather than trying to count phytoestrogens, therefore, the best approach is to become familiar with the foods that contain them and to aim to include these in your diet several times each day.

Should I take supplements?

In short, no. Despite the fact that some £64 million is spent on phytoestrogen supplements across Europe each year, studies have found that naturally-occurring phytoestrogens are far more effective than those presented as pills.

Reliability is also a problem. When phytoestrogen supplements have been analysed, over two-thirds have been found to contain fewer phytoestrogens than the amount claimed by the manufacturer. As a result, experts advise women to consume their phytoestrogens as foods, not pills.

One simple solution

To get 45 mg of phytoestrogens, you need three servings of a phytoestrogen-rich food each day. Try the following simple solution:

1 Two slices of a soya or linseed bread
2 One serving of a phyto-rich muesli
3 Use soya milk in your tea or coffee, or make a fruit smoothie with soya milk

right All beans and pulses contain phytoestrogens.

Great phytoestrogen-rich choices

Food	Phytoestrogens per 100 g	Average serving	Phytoestrogens per serving
Textured vegetable protein (TVP)	75 mg	75 g	56 mg
Tofu	13.5–67 mg	100 g	40 mg
Linseeds (flax)	60–370 mg	1 tablespoon	31 mg
Banana & Mango Smoothie (see page 42)		1 glass	30 mg
Soya beans	37 mg	3 tablespoons	28 mg
Soya flour	131–198 mg	1 tablespoon	25 mg

Food		Phytoestrogens per 100 g	Average serving	Phytoestrogens per serving
Soya milk		5–10 mg	250 ml glass	12.5–25 mg
Strawberry Muesli (see page 34)			1 bowl with 150 ml soya milk	20 mg
Miracle Bread (see page 132)			2 slices	12 mg
Tempeh		29–53 mg	25 g	10 mg
Soya cheese		6–31 mg	1 slice (50 g)	9 mg
Miso		45 mg	1 tablespoon	7 mg
Meat-free soya burgers		8–15 mg	1 burger (50 g)	6 mg

Food		Phytoestrogens per 100 g	Average serving	Phytoestrogens per serving
Blackberries		4 mg	100 g	4 mg
Gooseberries		3 mg	100 g	3 mg
China green tea/black tea		3 mg/1.1 mg	1 cup	3 mg/1.1 mg
Peas, lentils and split peas		3.28 mg	50 g	1.6 mg
Chianti/Cabernet Sauvignon wine		1.1 mg	125 ml glass	1.4 mg
Currants and raisins		2 mg	small handful (50 g)	1.0 mg
Brown rice		0.3 mg	100 g	0.3 mg

Lifestyle approaches to the menopause

There are a number of other changes you can make to reduce the severity of menopausal symptoms. These include:

- Avoid getting too warm by dressing in layers so you can easily add and remove them in response to different room temperatures
- Sleep in a cool room
- Keep your temperature down by avoiding hot drinks and hot soups
- Avoid triggers for hot flushes such as alcohol or spicy foods
- Develop effective ways of dealing with stress and learn to relax
- When a hot flush starts to develop, take slow, deep breaths which may lessen the severity
- Take regular moderate exercise
- Maintain a healthy body weight
- Have your blood pressure checked regularly
- If you have diabetes, ensure that your blood sugar control is good

Non-traditional therapies

There are many alternative therapies that may help to alleviate some of the stress of the menopause, including acupuncture, meditation, massage and other relaxation techniques. Although no scientific evidence exists to suggest that these work, they will certainly not harm, and some women report great benefit from them. Some women also try herbal supplements such as Black Cohosh, Dong Quai and Ginseng. Always talk to your doctor before embarking on any of these therapies.

below Remember to take time out for yourself and to relax.

Heart disease and the menopause

Increasing the risk
Other factors that increase your risk of heart disease include:
- smoking
- high blood pressure
- diabetes
- high blood cholesterol levels
- inactivity
- being overweight
- alcohol intake
- low intake of fruit and vegetables

below Oily fish are the richest source of omega 3 fatty acids. Try to eat some at least once a week.

It is a common but mistaken belief that heart disease affects men more than women. Heart disease is in fact the most common cause of death among both women and men in Western societies. During 2001, 126,000 women died of heart disease in the UK – that's 50,000 more than cancer, so this cannot be overlooked as a serious health concern.

Heart disease occurs as a result of two processes which develop gradually over many years. The first process, atherosclerosis, is a build-up of cholesterol in the outer walls of the blood vessels in the heart (similar to lime scale building up inside a pipe), which reduces blood flow. When the heart works harder during exertion or times of increased emotion, the amount of blood flowing may be too low to meet demand, resulting in pain (angina).

The second process, thrombosis, occurs if the cholesterol deposits crack, allowing a blood clot to form and block a blood vessel completely. This is what happens during a heart attack where the blood flow to part of the heart is cut off, resulting in permanent damage to that area of the heart.

Before the menopause, women are protected against heart disease by the hormone oestrogen. As the menopause progresses and oestrogen levels decline, the incidence of heart disease in women rapidly escalates and within a few years matches that of men.

Four steps to a healthy heart
1 Eat healthily Avoid eating too much saturated fat, eat plenty of fish, poultry, fruit and vegetables and maintain a healthy body weight.
2 Be more active Half an hour every day is enough to make a difference and it's easy to build into your daily routine. Start off gently and gradually build up.
3 Smoke-free From the moment you stop smoking your risk of heart attack starts to fall and is halved within one year of giving up.
4 Reduce your alcohol intake Binge drinking increases your risk of having a heart attack.

What affects your heart?

Negative factors

Low intake of fruit and vegetables Currently less than one in three people eat at least five portions a day. If we all ate five a day, the incidence of heart disease, stroke and cancers would fall by 20 per cent.

Saturated fats These are mainly found in animal foods such as butter, cream, lard, fatty meats, burgers, sausages, pies and pasties, but also in some vegetable sources, particularly palm oil and coconut. Choose lean cuts of meat and eat fewer processed meat products.

Adding extra fats Try to limit the amount of fat that you add to foods – spread margarine or butter thinly, choose tomato – rather than cream-based sauces and choose your cooking method carefully. Keep fried foods to a treat, roast without adding fat, stir-fry, boil or casserole.

Raised cholesterol levels Often caused by a diet high in saturated fats. If your cholesterol level is high, choose a cholesterol-lowering spread in place of butter or margarine.

Low-fibre diet This leaves you feeling hungry and constipated. Even slight constipation makes you feel sluggish and dull. Increasing fibre intake reduces fatigue and boosts energy levels by 10 per cent.

Weight gain Bad for your self-esteem and your general health. The most common cause is inactivity, so get out there and be as active as you can, as often as you can.

Positive factors

Antioxidants These hugely beneficial chemicals found in fruit and vegetables come in a wide range of colours, so try to eat fruit and vegetables of all colours and at least five portions every day. Also found in red wine and grape juice.

Polyunsaturated and monounsaturated fats These help to moderate cholesterol levels if eaten in moderation. They include olive, sunflower, soya, rapeseed and corn oils, and spreads or margarines made from these. Always use fats with moderation.

Soya and phytoestrogens Phytoestrogen-rich soya foods are proven to lower cholesterol levels and protect the heart. Try to include three servings of a soya food in your diet daily.

Oily fish Try to eat herring, mackerel, trout, salmon, pilchards or sardines once or twice every week.

High-fibre cereal foods These provide a long-lasting source of energy, keep you feeling full and offer a great source of dietary fibre, which helps to control cholesterol and blood sugar levels. Choose wholegrain breads, cereals and pasta as often as you can.

Increased activity This helps the heart and muscles get fitter, and boosts the metabolism, helping with weight control. It is the best form of stress relief, helps control anxiety and depression and is a fantastic mood-enhancer. If you want to feel and look great, get active.

Managing weight during the menopause

Around the time of the menopause, many women have problems maintaining their normal body weight. In fact, by the age of 55–64 years, three-quarters of women are overweight or obese. While there is no direct evidence that the menopause is a cause of weight gain in itself, the symptoms of the menopause may dampen your enthusiasm for exercise. Also, other lifestyle changes may be affecting both eating and activity levels, such as your children leaving home or a flush of cash due to the mortgage being paid off. It does not take much of an imbalance between energy intake and energy expenditure for weight to suddenly start creeping on.

below Remember to drink plenty of fluids to stave off hunger and flush away toxins.

Why worry about your weight?

It is uncomfortable to be large, but a more pressing concern is the impact

on your health. Carrying extra body fat places a strain on the heart, stresses the immune system, making you more susceptible to infections, makes you more likely to have joint problems and increases the risk of diseases such as diabetes, cancer, gallstones and heart disease. Important too is where you carry your weight. Weight around your middle is most damaging to health. For women, if your waist is bigger than 80 cm (31½ inches), then now is the time to take action. For men, a waist measurement greater than 94 cm (37 inches) requires a change in lifestyle.

While 'quick-fix' diets promising overnight weight loss are tempting, remember they are just that – a quick-fix that is temporary. The most effective approach to long-term weight control is a combination of healthy eating and increased activity levels.

Keeping active

Inactivity is the main cause of gradual weight gain. Only one-quarter of women achieve the recommended activity levels of 30 minutes of moderate activity per day. Becoming more active should be a major focus for anyone trying to manage their weight. And we are not just talking about getting down to the gym. How many hours each day do you spend sitting down? Think about all the times through the day that you could be more active – whether it is finding time for a quick walk, washing the car by hand instead of driving to the car wash, going bowling rather than spending another evening in front of the television or using the stairs instead of the lift.

It is surprising how quickly lots of little bits of extra activity through a day can add up to make you fitter and keep you burning off the calories. If you simply found the time to have a 20-minute brisk walk every day for a year, then you could burn off 5 kg (11 lb) of body fat. Not a huge amount of effort, but the potential for great results.

above Being active with friends is easier than going alone.

Keeping a diary

We often don't realize how much or how often we eat each day, or how inactive we actually are. Keeping a food and activity diary can be the prompt we need to become more aware of our habits and start to make changes to them. Try keeping a diary for a few days to become more aware of what you are doing at different times of day or in different situations.

Complete your diary as honestly as you can and then take a critical look at your habits. Consider the following.

- Are you eating regular meals – do you include breakfast every day?
- Are you eating at least five portions of fruit and vegetables every day?
- How often do you eat and drink between meals?
- Are there any times when you could be more active?
- Are there times when you choose not to be active?

Food and activity dairy

Time of day	What food or what activity?	How much?	Who with?	How I felt
Breakfast	Bowl of cereal with semi-skimmed milk and sugar 2 cups of tea	Medium bowl ⅓ pint 2 spoons 2 cups	The family	Rushed at the start of the day
Mid-morning	Cup of tea with a banana	1 cup 1 medium	Alone at my desk	Hungry
Lunch	Walking Sandwich made with reduced-fat cheese and tomatoes Cup of tea with milk	45 minutes 2 slices bread 2 slices cheese 5 cherry tomatoes 1 cup	A friend	Fabulous. Came back from the walk feeling hot but energized. Needed the sandwich and cup of tea afterwards, but felt alert for the rest of the day.

Making changes

After taking a careful look at your habits, now is the time to start making some changes. Setting yourself goals is easy – but achieving them is hard. This is often because the goals that we set are not achievable or simply the wrong ones. Goals should always be challenging enough to take us into new territory and to do things that we have not managed before – after all, what is the point of putting in all of the effort otherwise? However, we do need to make sure that they will give us the end results we want. Learning how to set goals that work takes practice and patience – we also need to learn from a few failures to get better at doing this.

The rules of SMART goals

Always make sure your goals include the following elements:

S – **Specific** What are you actually going to do? A specific goal would be to cut down the number of chips you eat from three servings a week to just one. A non-specific goal would be to 'eat fewer chips'.

M – **Measurable** Always include numbers in your goals so you know if you are successful. For example, walk for 20 minutes twice each week – you can easily see if you are achieving this goal.

A – **Achievable** A goal has to be tough but achievable. If at the moment you never go out for a walk, setting a goal to walk every day for an hour is going to be tough! Set something more realistic, such as walking twice a week. If you can do that, then make it more challenging.

R – **Realistic** Don't be scared to set small goals in order to work up to reaching a bigger goal that at the moment feels impossible. What will achieving the goal give you? The hardest goals will give you the greatest boost, so be realistic about the work involved, commit to doing it and then get going.

T – **Time specific** Set a time scale to review your goals every few weeks to see how you are getting on.

If you don't meet your goals

We need to accept that sometimes we will not achieve what we set out to do. If this is the case, then resist the temptation to be negative. All too often we assume that we are a failure, weak-willed and incapable of achieving success. There are lots of reasons why we fail to achieve – the trick is to use these occasions as a learning experience. Think about what you wanted to do. Was it SMART? How much of your goal did you manage to achieve and what went wrong? How could you do it differently next time?

Spend some time thinking about it rather than simply writing yourself off. Being able to set effective goals takes time and practice, and only by doing it will you become good at it. Above all, stick with it as the results are well worth achieving.

breakfasts

preparation time
15 minutes

cooking time
25–30 minutes

makes 6 muffins

nutritional values per muffin
- 250 kcals
- 10 g fat
- 2.5 g saturated fat
- 2.5 g fibre
- Source of phytoestrogens

Cook's tip
These muffins are best eaten fresh, but they will keep for 2–3 days in an airtight container.

banana muffins with cinnamon topping

butter, for greasing (optional)
100 g (3 1/2 oz) plain wholemeal flour
25 g (1 oz) soya flour
3 tablespoons light muscovado sugar
2 teaspoons baking powder
1 egg, beaten
50 ml (2 fl oz) soya milk
50 ml (2 fl oz) sunflower oil
2 ripe bananas, about 200 g (7 oz) when peeled, roughly mashed

Topping
1 tablespoon golden linseeds
25 g (1 oz) self-raising flour, sifted
15 g (1/2 oz) butter, at room temperature
40 g (1 1/2 oz) demerara sugar
1/2 teaspoon ground cinnamon
1 tablespoon water

As well as making a delicious breakfast, these tasty muffins make a great portable snack for when you are on the move.

1 Line 6 muffin tins with paper muffin cases or grease the tins well. Begin by making the topping. Place the linseeds in a blender or food processor and process for 30 seconds. Alternatively, grind them in a clean coffee grinder. Place the self-raising flour in a bowl and rub in the butter until the mixture resembles fine breadcrumbs. Add the sugar, linseeds and cinnamon, then stir in the measured water and mix well.

2 Place the wholemeal and soya flours, sugar and baking powder in a bowl, mix together and make a well in the centre. In a separate bowl, mix the egg, soya milk and oil together. Pour the liquid into the flour. Stir until just blended. Stir in the bananas, taking care not to overmix.

3 Fill the muffin cases or tins two-thirds full with the mixture, then sprinkle a little of the topping over each muffin. Place in a preheated oven at 200°C (400°F), Gas Mark 6, for 20–35 minutes, or until a skewer inserted into the centre comes out clean. Transfer the muffins to a wire rack to cool.

preparation time
10 minutes

cooking time
5 minutes

makes 10–12 servings

nutritional values per serving
- 364–304 kcals
- 26–17 g fat
- 10–6 g saturated fat
- 6–4 g fibre
- Source of phytoestrogens

Cook's tip
The granola can be stored in an airtight container for up to 1 month.

granola

75 g (3 oz) butter
5 tablespoons clear honey
1 teaspoon vanilla essence
300 g (10 oz) rolled oats
50 g (2 oz) dried shredded coconut
50 g (2 oz) flaked almonds
3 tablespoons sunflower seeds
3 tablespoons pumpkin seeds
1 tablespoon sesame seeds
1 tablespoon linseeds
75 g (3 oz) rye flakes
75 g (3 oz) ready-to-eat dried mixed fruit salad, roughly chopped

1 Place the butter, honey and vanilla essence in a small saucepan. Cook over a medium heat, stirring occasionally, for 5 minutes, or until the honey and butter are combined.

2 Place all the remaining ingredients, except the fruit, in a large bowl and mix well. Carefully stir in the butter mixture. Spread the mixture over the base of a large, nonstick roasting tin and place in a preheated oven at 160°C (325°F), Gas Mark 3, for 20 minutes, or until the grains are crisp and browned. Stir occasionally to prevent the mixture from sticking.

3 Remove from the oven and allow to cool. Stir in the dried fruit.

preparation time
5 minutes

cooking time
5–10 minutes

serves 2

nutritional values per serving
- 255 kcals
- 4 g fat
- 0.5 g saturated fat
- 3 g fibre
- Source of phytoestrogens

Cook's tip
Instead of bananas try adding a handful of fresh berries or a few roughly chopped ready-to-eat dried apricots.

banana porridge

75 g (3 oz) rolled oats
100 ml (3^1/$_2$ fl oz) soya milk
75 ml (3 fl oz) water
1 tablespoon brown sugar
1 large ripe banana, about 125 g (4 oz), peeled and finely sliced
To serve
extra soya milk
pumpkin seeds

1 Place the oats, soya milk, water, sugar and banana in a heavy-based saucepan. Bring to the boil, stirring steadily. Reduce the heat and simmer, stirring occasionally, for 5–10 minutes, or until the desired consistency is reached.

2 Spoon into bowls, pour over a little more soya milk and scatter over a few pumpkin seeds.

preparation time
5 minutes

cooking time
2–2^1/$_2$ hours

makes 12–14 servings

nutritional values per serving
- 229–200 kcals
- 12–10 g fat
- 1–0.7 g saturated fat
- 3–2.5 g fibre
- Source of phytoestrogens

Cook's tip
The muesli can be stored for up to about 3 weeks in an airtight container.

strawberry muesli

250 g (8 oz) strawberries, thinly sliced
250 g (8 oz) rolled oats
75 g (3 oz) flaked almonds
75 g (3 oz) pumpkin seeds
75 g (3 oz) sunflower seeds
25 g (1 oz) golden linseeds
75 g (3 oz) ready-to-eat dried cranberries, roughly chopped
soya milk, to serve

1 Blot away any juice from the strawberries with kitchen paper and lay them in a single layer on a baking tray lined with silicone paper. Place in a preheated oven at 110°C (225°F), Gas Mark ^{1}/$_4$, for 1 hour, turn over and continue to cook for a further 1–1^1/$_2$ hours, or until crisp. Allow to cool.

2 Mix together the remaining ingredients, carefully stir in the strawberries and store the mixture in an airtight container. When ready to serve, pour into bowls and add a splash of soya milk.

preparation time
5 minutes

serves 2

nutritional values per serving
- 300 kcals
- 11 g fat
- 1.5 g saturated fat
- 3 g fibre
- Source of phytoestrogens

lemon and passionfruit yogurt with muesli

2 tablespoons lemon curd
4 tablespoons Strawberry Muesli (see page 34), or other sugar-free muesli
400 ml (14 fl oz) plain soya yogurt
3 passionfruit

1 Stir the lemon curd and the muesli into the soya yogurt and spoon the mixture into 2 dishes. Remove the seeds and pulp from the passionfruit and drizzle over the yogurt. Serve immediately.

preparation time
10 minutes

cooking time
15 minutes

serves 2

nutritional values per serving
- 230 kcals
- 9 g fat
- 1 g saturated fat
- 2 g fibre
- Source of phytoestrogens

spiced apricots with yogurt

75 g (3 oz) ready-to-eat dried apricots,
roughly chopped
150 ml (1/4 pint) unsweetened
orange juice
1 cardamom pod, seeds removed and
lightly crushed
400 ml (14 fl oz) plain soya yogurt

1 Place the apricots, orange juice and crushed cardamom seeds in a small saucepan and gently heat. As soon as the orange juice begins to boil, reduce the heat, cover and simmer for 10 minutes.

2 Transfer the apricot mixture to a blender or food processor and purée until smooth, adding a little more juice if necessary. Allow the mixture to cool.

3 Stir the apricot purée into the soya yogurt and serve.

preparation time
5 minutes

cooking time
4–8 minutes

serves 2

nutritional values per serving
- 234 kcals
- 10 g fat
- 5 g saturated fat
- 2 g fibre
- Source of phytoestrogens

Cook's tip
If you like, try using Burgen bread for this recipe – it is also high in phytoestrogens.

pain perdu with fruit compôte

2 slices Miracle Bread (see page 132)
1 egg, beaten
3 tablespoons soya milk
1 drop vanilla extract, or a pinch of ground cinnamon
15 g (1/2 oz) butter
2 tablespoons golden caster sugar
Summer Fruit Compôte (see page 120), to serve

1 Cut the slices of bread in half diagonally. Beat together the egg, milk and vanilla or cinnamon. Heat the butter in a nonstick frying pan. Dip the bread slices in the egg mixture until well coated.

2 When the butter is foaming, add the bread and sprinkle over half the sugar. Fry over a medium heat for 2-3 minutes. Turn over, sprinkle with the remaining sugar and cook for a further 2 minutes.

3 Serve immediately with the fruit compôte.

preparation time
5 minutes

cooking time
2–3 minutes

serves 2

nutritional values per serving
- 211 kcals
- 12 g fat
- 5 g saturated fat
- 0 g fibre
- Good source of phytoestrogens

spiced chocolate milk

500 ml (17 fl oz) soya milk
50 g (2 oz) plain chocolate, grated
1 teaspoon clear honey
¼ teaspoon ground cardamom

1 Place the soya milk in a small saucepan and heat gently. Whisk in the remaining ingredients, then pour into mugs and serve immediately.

preparation time
5 minutes

cooking time
10 minutes

serves 2

nutritional values per serving
- 50 kcals
- 3 g fat
- 0.5 g saturated fat
- 0 g fibre
- Good source of phytoestrogens

Cook's tip
Fresh soya milk has a much better flavour than soya milk sold in long-life cartons.

almond soya latte

300 ml ($1/2$ pint) soya milk
4 drops of almond essence
150 ml ($1/4$ pint) hot espresso coffee
sugar, to taste

1 Place the soya milk in a saucepan and slowly bring to the boil, stirring occasionally. Pour the milk into two tall, heatproof glasses.

2 Add the almond essence to the coffee, then stir into the milk. Add sugar to taste and serve.

preparation time
2 minutes, plus freezing

serves 1

nutritional values per serving
- 230 kcals
- 3 g fat
- 0.5 g saturated fat
- 2 g fibre
- Good source of phytoestrogens

banana and mango smoothie

1 small ripe banana, about 100 g (3¹/₂ oz)
250 ml (8 fl oz) soya milk
1 small ripe mango, peeled, stoned and diced

1 Peel and slice the banana, then place in a freezerproof container and freeze for at least 2 hours or overnight.

2 Place all the ingredients in a blender or food processor and blend until thick and frothy. Pour into a glass and serve immediately.

light bites

preparation time
10 minutes

cooking time
10–15 minutes

serves 2

nutritional values per serving
- 440 kcals
- 23 g fat
- 4.5 g saturated fat
- 4.5 g fibre

Cook's tip
Give the potatoes a good wash but leave the skins on to increase the fibre.

cajun potato, prawn and avocado salad

300 g (10 oz) baby new potatoes, halved
1 tablespoon olive oil
250 g (8 oz) cooked peeled king prawns
I garlic clove, crushed
4 spring onions, finely sliced
2 teaspoons Cajun seasoning
1 ripe avocado, peeled, stoned and diced
handful of alfalfa sprouts
salt

1 Cook the potatoes in a large saucepan of lightly salted boiling water for 10–15 minutes, or until tender. Drain well.

2 Heat the oil in a wok or large, nonstick frying pan. Add the prawns, garlic, spring onions and Cajun seasoning, and stir-fry for 2–3 minutes, or until the prawns are hot. Stir in the potatoes and cook for a further 1 minute. Transfer to a serving dish.

3 Stir in the avocado, top with the alfalfa sprouts and serve.

preparation time
10 minutes

cooking time
5 minutes

serves 2

nutritional values per serving
- 320 kcals
- 29 g fat
- 5 g saturated fat
- 5 g fibre
- Source of phytoestrogens

green salad with toasted mixed seeds

1 tablespoon sunflower seeds
1 tablespoon pumpkin seeds
2 teaspoons sesame seeds
2 teaspoons golden linseeds
pinch of chilli flakes
2 tablespoons dark soy sauce
50 g (2 oz) mixed baby salad leaves
1/2 small cucumber, sliced
2 spring onions, finely chopped
1 small avocado, peeled, stoned and diced
Miracle Bread (see page 132), to serve

1 Place the seeds, chilli flakes and soy sauce in a bowl and mix well. Heat a small, heavy-based frying pan, add the seed mixture and cook for 5 minutes, stirring continuously.

2 Mix the remaining ingredients together in a serving bowl, sprinkle with the seed mixture and serve with Miracle Bread.

preparation time
10 minutes

cooking time
10–15 minutes

serves 2

nutritional values per serving
- 250 kcals
- 14 g fat
- 1 g saturated fat
- 8 g fibre
- Source of phytoestrogens

tuna and flageolet bean salad

300 g (10 oz) canned flageolet beans, drained and rinsed
4 vine-ripened tomatoes, quartered
4 spring onions, finely chopped
185 g (6$^1/_2$ oz) canned tuna in spring water, drained and flaked
12 pitted black olives, roughly chopped
handful of flat leaf parsley, roughly chopped
handful of rocket leaves
Miracle Bread (see page 132), to serve

Dressing
2 tablespoons extra virgin olive oil
1 tablespoon white wine vinegar
pinch of mustard powder
pinch of caster sugar
$^1/_4$ teaspoon crushed garlic
salt and freshly ground black pepper

1 Place the beans, tomatoes, spring onions, tuna, olives, parsley and rocket in a serving bowl and toss together.

2 Place all the dressing ingredients in a screw-top jar and shake vigorously to dissolve the sugar. Add the dressing to the salad and toss well to coat. Serve with Miracle Bread.

preparation time
10 minutes

cooking time
5 minutes

serves 2

nutritional values per serving
- 350 kcals
- 15 g fat
- 3 g saturated fat
- 8 g fibre
- Source of phytoestrogens

smoked chicken salad

150 g (5 oz) asparagus, cut into 5 cm (2 inch) lengths
200 g (7 oz) smoked chicken breast, cut into bite-sized pieces
125 g (4 oz) cherry tomatoes, halved
300 g (10 oz) canned cannellini beans, drained and rinsed
handful of chives, chopped
Dressing
2 tablespoons olive oil
1 garlic clove, crushed
2 teaspoons clear honey
2 teaspoons balsamic vinegar
2 teaspoons wholegrain mustard

1 Cook the asparagus in a large saucepan of lightly salted boiling water for about 4 minutes, or until just tender. Drain and plunge into cold water to prevent it cooking further. Pat dry with kitchen paper.

2 Place the chicken in a large bowl, add the tomatoes, beans, asparagus and chives and mix well.

3 To make the dressing, whisk all the ingredients together in a small bowl. Pour the dressing over the salad and toss well to coat.

Variation
If you can't find smoked chicken, use ordinary cooked chicken breast and chargrill the asparagus to add more flavour. Cook the asparagus in a large saucepan of lightly salted boiling water for 2–3 minutes. Drain well and pat dry with kitchen paper. Toss the asparagus with 1 tablespoon of olive oil and place on a hot griddle pan for 2–3 minutes, turning once, or until charred. Continue with Step 2 of the main recipe.

preparation time
10 minutes

cooking time
6–10 minutes

serves 2

nutritional values per serving
- 524 kcals
- 16 g fat
- 2 g saturated fat
- 10 g fibre
- Source of phytoestrogens

falafel with salad and pitta breads

400 g (13 oz) canned chickpeas, drained and rinsed
1 garlic clove, crushed
2 tablespoons chopped fresh coriander
1 small red onion, roughly chopped
$^1/_2$ teaspoon ground cumin
$^1/_2$ teaspoon ground turmeric
1 tablespoon tahini
$^1/_2$ teaspoon salt
25 g (1 oz) fresh white breadcrumbs
2 tablespoons water
plain flour, for shaping
vegetable oil, for frying
To serve
2 wholemeal pitta breads, toasted
mixed salad
Tofu and Garlic Dip (see page 56)

1 Place the chickpeas, garlic, coriander, onion, spices, tahini, salt and breadcrumbs in a blender or food processor and process until finely chopped. Turn the mixture into a large bowl and add the measured water. Knead the mixture with your hands until it binds together, adding a little more water if necessary.

2 With floured hands, shape the mixture into 6 small patties. Heat 2.5 cm (1 inch) of vegetable oil in a large, deep frying pan and fry the patties in batches for 2–3 minutes on each side. Drain on kitchen paper.

3 To serve, split open the toasted pitta breads to make pockets. Fill with the falafel, plenty of mixed salad and a tablespoon of Tofu and Garlic Dip.

preparation time
10 minutes

cooking time
10 minutes

serves 2

nutritional values per serving
- 265 kcals
- 10 g fat
- 1.5 g saturated fat
- 8 g fibre
- Source of phytoestrogens

Cook's tip
To skin tomatoes, place in a heatproof bowl, cover with boiling water and leave to stand for 1 minute. Plunge the tomatoes into a bowl of ice-cold water. Peel off the skins.

spiced chickpea salad

1 tablespoon olive oil
1 red onion, finely chopped
1 teaspoon ground turmeric
2 teaspoons cumin seeds
300 g (10 oz) tomatoes, skinned and roughly chopped
400 g (13 oz) canned chickpeas, drained and rinsed
2 teaspoons lemon juice
2 tablespoons chopped fresh coriander
salt and freshly ground black pepper
Miracle Bread (see page 132), to serve

1 Heat the oil in a heavy-based saucepan, add the onion and sauté for 5 minutes, or until softened.

2 Add the turmeric and cumin seeds and cook, stirring, for 1–2 minutes. Add the tomatoes, chickpeas, lemon juice and seasoning and cook for a further 2–3 minutes.

3 Stir in the chopped coriander and serve with Miracle Bread.

preparation time	nutritional values per serving	Cook's tip

preparation time
5 minutes

serves 2–3

nutritional values per serving
- 260–170 kcals
- 11–7 g fat
- 1–0.5 g saturated fat
- 8–5.5 g fibre
- Source of phytoestrogens

Cook's tip
You can use other canned beans in place of the butter beans, such as cannellini or red kidney beans.

butter bean, anchovy and coriander pâté

425 g (14 oz) canned butter beans, drained and rinsed
50 g (2 oz) canned anchovy fillets in oil
2 spring onions, finely chopped
2 tablespoons lemon juice
1 tablespoon olive oil
4 tablespoons chopped fresh coriander
salt and freshly ground black pepper
To serve
lemon wedges
toasted rye bread

Serve this flavoursome pâté on toasted rye bread or Miracle Bread (see page 132).

1 Place all the ingredients, except the coriander, in a blender or food processor. Purée until well mixed but not smooth. Alternatively, mash the beans with a fork, finely chop the anchovies and mix the ingredients together by hand.

2 Stir in the coriander and season well. Serve with lemon wedges and toasted rye bread.

preparation time
5 minutes

serves 4

nutritional values per serving
- 111 kcals
- 9 g fat
- 1 g saturated fat
- 0 g fibre
- Good source of phytoestrogens

tofu and garlic dip

325 g (11 oz) silken tofu
2 tablespoons extra virgin olive oil
2 large garlic cloves, crushed
1 teaspoon Dijon mustard
1^1/$_2$ tablespoons lemon juice
freshly ground black pepper

To serve
breadsticks
crudités

Serve this smooth, tangy dip with breadsticks and/or vegetable crudités, such as carrot, cucumber, red pepper and celery.

1 Place all the ingredients in a blender or food processor and purée until smooth. Season well with pepper.

2 Cover and chill until ready to serve. Serve with breadsticks and crudités.

preparation time
5 minutes

cooking time
15 minutes, plus cooling

serves 2

nutritional values per serving
- 180 kcals
- 14 g fat
- 2 g saturated fat
- 2 g fibre
- Good source of phytoestrogens

spicy red pepper dip

1 large red pepper, about 150 g (5 oz)

150 g (5 oz) silken tofu

2 tablespoons olive oil

1 tablespoon sweet chilli sauce

4 tablespoons hot water

salt and freshly ground black pepper

crudités, such as carrot and cucumber,
to serve

1 Slice the pepper in half and place, cut-side down, under a preheated hot grill until the skin is blackened and the flesh soft. Place the pepper halves in a plastic bag and allow to cool for 15 minutes.

2 Skin, core and deseed the peppers, then place the flesh in a blender or food processor with the tofu, oil and chilli sauce. Blend for 1 minute, then add the measured water and purée until smooth. Season well with salt and pepper.

3 Cover and chill for at least 2 hours to allow the flavours to develop. Taste and adjust the seasoning if necessary, then serve with crudités.

preparation time
15 minutes

cooking time
10 minutes

serves 2

nutritional values per serving
● 300 kcals
● 14 g fat
● 7 g saturated fat
● 8 g fibre
● Source of phytoestrogens

seared scallops with minted bean purée

15 g (1/2 oz) butter
2 shallots or 1/2 small onion, finely chopped
300 g (10 oz) canned broad beans, drained, rinsed and outer shells removed
1 teaspoon mint sauce
6 tablespoons reduced-fat crème fraîche
10 large scallops, shelled and cleaned
1 tablespoon olive oil
extra virgin olive oil, to drizzle
salt and freshly ground black pepper
mint sprigs, to garnish

1 Melt the butter in small saucepan and cook the shallots or onion over a medium heat for 5 minutes, or until softened. Place the shallots, beans, mint sauce and crème fraîche in a blender or food processor and blend to make a coarse purée. Season to taste, then place in a clean saucepan and gently heat.

2 Brush the scallops with the olive oil, place on a hot griddle pan and sear for 2 minutes on each side, or until browned and cooked through.

3 To serve, spoon a mound of bean purée on to 2 large white plates, and arrange 5 scallops around the edge of each plate. Drizzle with the extra virgin olive oil and garnish with mint sprigs and a grinding of black pepper.

preparation time
10 minutes

cooking time
5 minutes

serves 2

nutritional values per serving
- 350 kcals
- 20 g fat
- 3 g saturated fat
- 8 g fibre
- Source of phytoestrogens

hummus with dukkha

400 g (13 oz) canned chickpeas, drained and rinsed
1 tablespoon tahini
2 tablespoons olive oil
2 garlic cloves, crushed
4 tablespoons lemon juice
3 tablespoons hot water
wholemeal pitta bread, toasted, to serve

Dukkha
2 tablespoons sesame seeds
1 tablespoon cumin seeds
$1/2$ tablespoon ground coriander
25 g (1 oz) hazelnuts, finely chopped
$1/4$ teaspoon salt

Dukkha is an Egyptian spice mix made from a blend of nuts and seeds. It can be scattered over salads, used to top fish or served as a nibble with a small dish of extra virgin olive oil and hot bread.

1 To make the pâté, place the chickpeas, tahini, oil, garlic, lemon juice and measured water in a blender or food processor and process until smooth. Alternatively, mash the ingredients together with a fork.

2 To make the dukkha, toast the sesame and cumin seeds and coriander in a dry frying pan over a low heat for 3 minutes, moving them about until they start to smell fragrant. Tip them out on to a plate. Add the hazelnuts to the frying pan and fry for 1–2 minutes, or until lightly golden. Stir the nuts and salt into the seed mixture. Store in an airtight container for up to 1 week.

3 Spread the pâté on wholemeal pitta bread and sprinkle with a little of the dukkha.

preparation time
15 minutes

cooking time
25 minutes

serves 2

nutritional values per serving
- 280 kcals
- 7 g fat
- 1 g saturated fat
- 11 g fibre
- Source of phytoestrogens

boston baked beans

1 tablespoon vegetable oil
1 small red onion, finely chopped
2 celery sticks, finely chopped
1 garlic clove, crushed
200 g (7 oz) canned chopped tomatoes
150 ml ($\frac{1}{4}$ pint) vegetable stock
1 tablespoon dark soy sauce
1 tablespoon dark brown sugar
2 teaspoons Dijon mustard
400 g (13 oz) canned mixed beans, drained and rinsed
2 tablespoons chopped parsley

Real homemade baked beans are a revelation. Serve on toasted seed bread for a light meal, or use as an accompaniment to sausages or grilled meat.

1 Heat the oil in heavy-based saucepan. Add the onion and cook over a low heat for 5 minutes, or until softened. Add the celery and garlic and continue to cook for 1–2 minutes.

2 Add the tomatoes, stock and soy sauce. Bring to the boil, then reduce to a fast simmer and cook for about 15 minutes, or until the sauce begins to thicken.

3 Add the sugar, mustard and beans. Continue to cook for a further 5 minutes, or until the beans are heated through. Stir in the chopped parsley and serve.

preparation time
10 minutes, plus draining

cooking time
10 minutes

serves 2

nutritional values per serving
- 250 kcals
- 8 g fat
- 1 g saturated fat
- 0.5 g fibre
- Good source of phytoestrogens

fragrant tofu and noodle soup

125 g (4 oz) firm tofu, diced
1 tablespoon sesame oil
75 g (3 oz) thin rice noodles
600 ml (1 pint) vegetable stock
2.5 cm (1 inch) piece of fresh root ginger, peeled and thickly sliced
1 large garlic clove, thickly sliced
3 kaffir lime leaves, torn in half
2 lemon grass stalks, halved
handful of spinach or pak choi leaves
50 g (2 oz) bean sprouts
1–2 fresh red chillies, deseeded and finely sliced
2 tablespoons fresh coriander
1 tablespoon Thai fish sauce

To serve
lime wedges
chilli sauce

1 Place the tofu on a plate covered with kitchen paper and allow to stand for 10 minutes to drain.

2 Heat the oil in a wok or frying pan until hot, add the tofu and cook for 2–3 minutes, stirring, or until the tofu is golden brown. Remove from the pan and drain on kitchen paper.

3 Meanwhile, soak the noodles in boiling water for 2 minutes, then drain.

4 Place the stock in a large saucepan. Add the ginger, garlic, lime leaves and lemon grass and bring to the boil. Reduce the heat, add the tofu, noodles, spinach or pak choi, bean sprouts and chillies and heat through for a couple of minutes. Stir in the coriander and the Thai fish sauce, then pour into warmed deep soup bowls to serve. Serve with lime wedges and chilli sauce.

preparation time
10 minutes

cooking time
40 minutes

serves 4

nutritional values per serving
- 230 kcals
- 4 g fat
- 0.4 g saturated fat
- 12 g fibre
- Source of phytoestrogens

Cook's tip
Rinsing canned beans will help to remove some of the sugars that can cause wind. Vitamin C in an accompanying glass of fruit juice will help your body absorb the iron from the beans.

Tuscan bean soup

1 tablespoon olive oil
1 small red onion, finely chopped
1 garlic clove, finely chopped
1 carrot, diced
2 celery sticks, chopped
400 g (13 oz) canned chopped tomatoes
1 tablespoon sun-dried tomato paste
600 ml (1 pint) vegetable stock
750 g (1¹/₂ lb) canned mixed beans, drained and rinsed
3 tablespoons chopped flat leaf parsley
salt and freshly ground black pepper
ready-made fresh pesto, to serve

1 Heat the oil in a heavy-based saucepan and sauté the onion for about 5 minutes, or until softened. Stir in the garlic, carrot and celery and continue to cook for a further 5 minutes.

2 Add the tomatoes, tomato paste, stock and seasoning. Bring to the boil, then reduce the heat and simmer, stirring occasionally, for 20–30 minutes, or until the vegetables are soft.

3 Place half of the vegetable mixture into a blender or food processor and blend until smooth, then return to the pan. Add the beans and simmer for a further 10 minutes, or until the beans have been heated through. Just before serving, stir in the chopped parsley. Serve in warmed soup bowls, garnished with a spoonful of pesto.

preparation time
15 minutes

cooking time
40 minutes

serves 2

nutritional values per serving
- 262 kcals
- 7 g fat
- 1 g saturated fat
- 5 g fibre
- Source of phytoestrogens

Cook's tip
Red lentils, often available in split form, do not need presoaking, only rinsing. Yellow lentils could be used in the same way instead.

curried lentil soup

1 tablespoon vegetable oil
1 small onion, finely chopped
1 garlic clove, crushed
1 small potato, finely diced
1 carrot, finely diced
2 celery sticks, finely chopped
1 tablespoon mild curry paste
50 g (2 oz) red lentils
200 g (7 oz) canned chopped tomatoes
600 ml (1 pint) chicken or vegetable stock
salt and freshly ground black pepper
chopped fresh coriander, to garnish

1 Heat the oil in large saucepan, add the onion and cook over a medium heat for 5 minutes, or until beginning to soften. Add the garlic, potato, carrot, celery and curry paste and continue to cook, stirring occasionally, for a further 5 minutes.

2 Add the lentils, tomatoes, stock and seasoning and bring the mixture to the boil. Reduce the heat, cover and simmer for 30 minutes, or until the lentils are soft.

3 Garnish with a little chopped coriander before serving.

preparation time
10 minutes

cooking time
20 minutes

serves 4

nutritional values per serving
- 250 kcals
- 12 g fat
- 4 g saturated fat
- 6 g fibre

pea, lettuce and lemon soup with sesame croûtons

25 g (1 oz) butter
1 large onion, finely chopped
425 g (14 oz) frozen peas
2 Little Gem lettuces, roughly chopped
1 litre (1³/4 pints) vegetable or chicken stock
grated rind and juice of ¹/2 lemon
salt and freshly ground black pepper

Sesame croûtons
2 thick slices of Miracle Bread (see page 132), cubed
1 tablespoon olive oil
1 tablespoon sesame seeds

1 To make the croûtons, brush the bread cubes with the oil and place in a roasting tin. Sprinkle with the sesame seeds and cook in a preheated oven at 200°C (400°F), Gas Mark 6, for 10–15 minutes, or until golden.

2 Meanwhile, heat the butter in a large saucepan, add the onion and cook for 5 minutes, or until beginning to soften. Add the peas, lettuce, stock, lemon rind and juice and seasoning. Bring to the boil, then reduce the heat, cover and simmer for 10–15 minutes.

3 Allow the soup to cool slightly, then transfer to a blender or food processor and purée until smooth. Return the soup to the pan, adjust the seasoning if necessary and heat through. Spoon into warmed serving bowls and sprinkle with the sesame croûtons.

preparation time
15 minutes

cooking time
10–15 minutes

serves 4

nutritional values per serving
- 200 kcals
- 14 g fat
- 2 g saturated fat
- 2 g fibre
- Good source of phytoestrogens

curried tofu burgers

Serve these spicy burgers in wholemeal rolls or pitta breads with plenty of crisp lettuce and onion rings.

1 tablespoon vegetable oil, plus extra for frying
1 large carrot, coarsely grated
1 small red onion, finely chopped
1 garlic clove, crushed
1 teaspoon hot curry paste
1 teaspoon sun-dried tomato paste
250 g (8 oz) firm tofu, drained
25 g (1 oz) wholemeal breadcrumbs
25 g (1 oz) unsalted peanuts, finely chopped
plain flour, for dusting
vegetable oil, for frying
salt and freshly ground black pepper

1 Heat the oil in a large, nonstick frying pan. Add the carrot and onion and fry for 3–4 minutes, or until the vegetables are softened, stirring constantly. Add the garlic and curry and tomato pastes. Increase the heat and fry for 2 minutes, stirring all the time.

2 Place the tofu, vegetables, breadcrumbs and nuts in a blender or food processor and process until just blended. Season well and beat until the mixture starts to stick together.

3 With floured hands, shape the mixture into 4 burgers. Heat a little oil in a large, nonstick frying pan and fry the burgers for 3–4 minutes on each side, or until golden brown. Alternatively, to grill the burgers, brush them with a little oil and cook under a preheated hot grill for about 3 minutes on each side, or until golden brown. Drain on kitchen paper and serve.

preparation time
15 minutes

cooking time
10 minutes

serves 2

nutritional values per serving
- 238 kcals
- 2 g fat
- 0.5 g saturated fat
- 14 g fibre
- Good source of phytoestrogens

spiced cannellini beans

2 teaspoons cumin seeds
1 red onion, finely chopped
about 8 tablespoons vegetable stock
1 green chilli, deseeded and finely chopped
2 garlic cloves, crushed
300 g (10 oz) ripe tomatoes, peeled and chopped
2 tablespoons sun-dried tomato paste
400 g (13 oz) canned cannellini beans, drained and rinsed
75 g (3 oz) spinach leaves
salt and freshly ground black pepper
toasted Miracle Bread (see page 132), to serve

1 Toast the cumin seeds in a dry, heavy-based saucepan until fragrant, then add the onion and 2 tablespoons of the stock. Gently cook for 5 minutes, adding extra stock as necessary. Add the chilli and garlic and dry-fry for a further 1 minute.

2 Stir in the tomatoes, tomato paste, beans and 4 tablespoons of the stock. Bring to the boil, then reduce the heat and simmer for 5 minutes.

3 Season well and stir in the spinach, then remove from the heat. Stir until the spinach has just wilted. Serve with toast.

preparation time
15 minutes

cooking time
8–10 minutes

serves 2

nutritional values per serving
- 235 kcals
- 11 g fat
- 2 g saturated fat
- 2 g fibre
- Good source of phytoestrogens

tofu kebabs with barbecue sauce

2 tablespoons dark soy sauce
2 tablespoons tomato purée
2 tablespoons clear honey
1 tablespoon white wine vinegar
1 garlic clove, finely chopped
1 tablespoon sesame oil
250 g (8 oz) firm tofu, cut into 2.5 cm (1 inch) cubes
2 courgettes, sliced into 2.5 cm (1 inch) slices
6 spring onions, cut into 5 cm (2 in) lengths

1 To make the marinade, mix the soy sauce, tomato purée, honey, vinegar, garlic and oil together in a large bowl. Brush the marinade over the tofu. Soak 4 bamboo skewers in cold water for 30 minutes.

2 Thread the tofu, courgettes and spring onions on to the skewers. Place the kebabs under a preheated hot grill for 4–5 minutes, turn and continue to cook for a further 4–5 minutes, or until cooked through and lightly charred.

preparation time
15 minutes

cooking time
30 minutes

serves 2

nutritional values per serving
- 370 kcals
- 16 g fat
- 4 g saturated fat
- 9 g fibre
- Source of phytoestrogens

Cook's tip
For a speedier dish, replace the dry lentils with 400 g (13 oz) canned lentils. Rinse and drain the lentils, then start the recipe from Step 2.

lentils with broad beans, bacon and poached egg

75 g (3 oz) Puy lentils
1 thyme sprig
1 celery stick
1 garlic clove
1 litre (1³/4 pints) water
3 rashers of smoked back bacon, roughly chopped
1 tablespoon olive oil
4 spring onions, finely sliced
200 g (7 oz) frozen broad beans, blanched and outer skins removed
1 tablespoon balsamic vinegar
2 eggs
salt and freshly ground black pepper

1 Place the lentils, thyme, celery and garlic in a saucepan and pour over the measured water. Bring to the boil, then reduce the heat and simmer for 20 minutes until tender. Drain the lentils and discard the thyme, celery and garlic.

2 Fry the bacon in the oil for 2–3 minutes, then add the spring onions and broad beans and fry for a further 2–3 minutes. Add the lentils and continue to cook for 1 minute. Season to taste and stir in the vinegar.

3 Meanwhile, poach the eggs in simmering water for just a couple of minutes. Remove with a slotted spoon and drain on kitchen paper. Divide the lentil mixture between 2 plates and top each mound with a poached egg. Serve immediately.

main dishes

preparation time
15 minutes

cooking time
30 minutes

serves 2

nutritional values per serving
- 500 kcals
- 23 g fat
- 6 g saturated fat
- 11 g fibre
- Source of phytoestrogens

Cook's tip
Use Miracle Bread (see page 132) or another bread rich in phytoestrogens to make the breadcrumbs.

spicy sausage cassoulet

1 tablespoon olive oil
1 red onion, finely chopped
1 garlic clove, crushed
1 red pepper, cored, deseeded and roughly chopped
2 celery sticks, roughly chopped
200 g (7 oz) canned chopped tomatoes
125 ml (4 fl oz) chicken stock
2 teaspoons dark soy sauce
1 teaspoon Dijon mustard
400 g (14 oz) canned black-eyed beans, drained and rinsed
125 g (4 oz) reduced-fat smoked pork sausage, roughly chopped
50 g (2 oz) fresh breadcrumbs
25 g (1 oz) freshly grated Parmesan
2 tablespoons chopped parsley
crisp green salad, to serve

1 Heat 2 teaspoons of the oil in a large, nonstick saucepan or wok, add the onion, garlic, red pepper and celery and cook over a low heat, stirring occasionally, for 3–4 minutes.

2 Add the tomatoes, stock and soy sauce. Bring to the boil, then reduce the heat and simmer for about 15 minutes, or until the sauce begins to thicken. Add the mustard, beans and sausage and continue to cook for a further 10 minutes.

2 Mix the breadcrumbs, Parmesan and parsley together and sprinkle over the sausage mixture. Drizzle over the remaining oil and place under a preheated medium-hot grill for 2–3 minutes, or until golden brown. Serve with a crisp green salad.

preparation time
15 minutes

cooking time
10–15 minutes

serves 2

nutritional values per serving
- 450 kcals
- 24 g fat
- 5 g saturated fat
- 2 g fibre
- Source of phytoestrogens

chicken and sesame goujons

75 g (3 oz) fresh breadcrumbs
2 tablespoons sesame seeds
2 large boneless, skinless chicken
breasts, cut into bite-sized pieces
1 egg, beaten
salt and freshly ground black pepper
olive oil spray
To serve
Spicy Red Pepper Dip (see page 57)
crunchy mixed salad

1 Mix the breadcrumbs, sesame seeds and seasoning together and spread over a large plate or baking tray. Dip the chicken pieces in the beaten egg, then roll in the breadcrumb mixture to coat thoroughly. Carefully lay the chicken on a lightly greased baking sheet and chill for 30 minutes.

2 Spray the chicken pieces with the olive oil spray and cook in a preheated oven at 200°C (400°F), Gas Mark 6, for 10–15 minutes, or until the breadcrumbs are golden brown and the chicken is cooked through. Serve with Spicy Red Pepper Dip and a large crunchy salad.

preparation time
15 minutes

cooking time
30–35 minutes

serves 2

nutritional values per serving
- 490 kcals
- 14 g fat
- 4 g saturated fat
- 5 g fibre
- Source of phytoestrogens

chicken and lemon paella

4 teaspoons olive oil
300 g (10 oz) boneless, skinless chicken thighs, diced
1 onion, sliced
2 garlic cloves, crushed
1 red pepper, cored, deseeded and roughly chopped
75 g (3 oz) easy-cook white long-grain rice
2 tablespoons sherry
250 ml (8 fl oz) chicken stock
200 g (7 oz) frozen peas
grated rind and juice of 1 lemon
salt and freshly ground black pepper
thyme sprigs, to garnish
lemon wedges, to serve

1 Heat 2 teaspoons of the oil in a frying pan over a medium heat and cook the chicken for 4–6 minutes, or until golden. Remove from the pan and add the remaining oil. Add the onion and cook over a medium heat for 10 minutes until soft. Add the garlic and red pepper and cook for a further 3 minutes.

2 Stir in the rice and pour in the sherry and stock. Return the chicken to the pan. Turn the heat to low and cook for 10–15 minutes.

3 Add the peas and cook for a further 2–3 minutes, or until the liquid has evaporated. Stir in the lemon rind and juice, then season to taste. Serve garnished with thyme sprigs, accompanied by lemon wedges.

preparation time
15 minutes, plus marinating

cooking time
1 1/2 hours

serves 2

nutritional values per serving
- 490 kcals
- 20 g fat
- 6 g saturated fat
- 8 g fibre
- Source of phytoestrogens

moroccan lamb

1 teaspoon ground ginger
1 teaspoon ground cumin
1 teaspoon paprika
1 cinnamon stick
50 ml (2 fl oz) orange juice
250 g (8 oz) lean lamb, cut into 5 cm (2 inch) cubes
125 g (4 oz) button onions or shallots, unpeeled
1 tablespoon olive oil
1 garlic clove, crushed
2 teaspoons flour
2 teaspoons tomato purée
125 ml (4 fl oz) lamb stock
3 tablespoons sherry
50 g (2 oz) ready-to-eat dried apricots
300 g (10 oz) canned chickpeas, drained and rinsed
salt and freshly ground black pepper
couscous, to serve

1 Place the spices in a large bowl and pour over the orange juice. Add the lamb and mix well, cover and leave in a cool place for at least 1 hour, or preferably overnight.

2 Place the onions or shallots in a saucepan of boiling water and cook for 2 minutes. Drain and refresh under cold water, then peel.

3 Heat the oil in a large, flameproof casserole. Remove the lamb from the marinade and brown over a high heat until golden all over. Using a slotted spoon, remove the lamb and set aside. Reduce the heat slightly and, adding a little more oil if necessary, cook the onions or shallots and garlic for 3 minutes, or until just beginning to brown. Return the meat to the pan and stir in the flour and tomato purée. Continue to cook for 1 minute.

4 Add the marinade to the pan with the stock, sherry and seasoning. Bring to the boil, then reduce the heat, cover and place in a preheated oven at 180°C (350°F), Gas Mark 4, for 1 hour. Add the apricots and chickpeas and return to the oven for a further 15 minutes. Serve with couscous cooked according to the packet instructions.

preparation time
15 minutes

cooking time
45 minutes

serves 2

nutritional values per serving
● 480 kcals
● 18 g fat
● 6g saturated fat
● 12 g fibre
● Good source of phytoestrogens

chilli con carne

1 tablespoon vegetable oil
1 red onion, finely chopped
1 garlic clove, finely chopped
250 g (8 oz) extra lean minced beef
1 small red pepper, cored, deseeded and diced
400 g (13 oz) canned chopped tomatoes
1 tablespoon tomato purée
2 teaspoons chilli powder
200 ml (7 fl oz) beef stock
400 g (13 oz) canned red kidney beans, drained and rinsed
salt and freshly ground black pepper
brown rice, to serve

1 Heat the oil in heavy-based, nonstick saucepan. Add the onion and garlic and cook for 5 minutes, or until beginning to soften. Add the mince and cook for a further 5–6 minutes, or until browned all over.

2 Stir in the red pepper, tomatoes, tomato purée, chilli powder and stock and bring to the boil. Reduce the heat and simmer gently for 30 minutes.

3 Add the beans and cook for a further 5 minutes. Season to taste and serve with brown rice, cooked according to the packet instructions.

preparation time
15 minutes

cooking time
20 minutes

serves 2

nutritional values per serving
- 530 kcals
- 18 g fat
- 8 g saturated fat
- 10 g fibre
- Source of phytoestrogens

Cook's tip
Arborio rice is used to make risotto because it absorbs more liquid and releases more starch than other types of rice, producing a creamy, velvety result.

broad bean and bacon risotto

300 g (10 oz) frozen broad beans
15 g ($^1/_2$ oz) butter
1 onion, finely chopped
4 rashers of rindless smoked back bacon, roughly chopped
125 g (4 oz) arborio rice
500 ml (17 fl oz) hot chicken stock
25 g (1 oz) freshly grated Parmesan
salt and freshly ground black pepper
Parmesan shavings, to garnish

1 Cook the broad beans in a saucepan of lightly salted boiling water for 2–3 minutes. Drain and plunge into ice-cold water to cool. Peel away and discard the outer shells and set the beans aside.

2 Heat the butter in a heavy-based saucepan. Add the onion and bacon and cook over a low heat for 5 minutes. Add the rice and beans and continue to cook, stirring, for 1–2 minutes.

3 Add just enough hot stock to cover the rice and continue to cook, stirring frequently, until most of the stock has been absorbed. Continue adding the stock in this way until it is almost completely absorbed and the rice is tender.

4 Remove from the heat, stir in the grated Parmesan and season to taste. Serve immediately, garnished with Parmesan shavings.

preparation time
10 minutes

cooking time
10–15 minutes

serves 2

nutritional values per serving
- 350 kcals
- 11 g fat
- 4 g saturated fat
- 9 g fibre
- Source of phytoestrogens

monkfish brochettes with cannellini beans and pesto

250 g (8 oz) monkfish, cut into 6 pieces
6 slices of Parma ham
6 cherry tomatoes
1 yellow pepper, cored, deseeded and cut into 6 pieces
1 tablespoon olive oil
300 g (10 oz) canned cannellini beans, drained and rinsed
2 tablespoons ready-made fresh pesto

1 Wrap each piece of monkfish in a slice of Parma ham. Thread on to 2 skewers, alternating with tomatoes and yellow pepper pieces. Brush the kebabs with the oil and cook under a preheated hot grill for 3–4 minutes. Turn and cook for a further 3 minutes until cooked through.

2 Place the beans in a nonstick saucepan and cook, stirring, over a low heat for 4–5 minutes, or until hot. Stir in the pesto. Spoon the beans on to 2 plates, top with the brochettes and serve immediately.

preparation time
15 minutes

cooking time
40–50 minutes

serves 2

nutritional values per serving
- 456 kcals
- 22 g fat
- 4 g saturated fat
- 6 g fibre
- Source of phytoestrogens

Cook's tip
If time is short, use a 400 g (13 oz) can of lentils in place of the dried in Step 2. Add to the Worcestershire sauce, tomatoes and coriander.

seared salmon on a bed of lentils

1 tablespoon olive oil
1 small onion, finely chopped
1 garlic clove, finely chopped
1 fennel bulb, chopped
100 g (3^1/2 oz) Puy lentils, washed
300 ml (^{1}/2 pint) chicken or vegetable stock
1 tablespoon Worcestershire sauce
12 small cherry tomatoes, halved
3 tablespoons chopped fresh coriander
2 salmon fillets, about 150 g (5 oz) each
salt and freshly ground black pepper

1 Heat the oil in a deep, nonstick frying pan. Add the onion, garlic and fennel and cook, stirring, for about 10 minutes, or until soft.

2 Add the lentils and stock and bring to the boil, then reduce the heat and simmer for 30–40 minutes, or until the lentils are tender. Stir in the Worcestershire sauce, tomatoes and coriander, and season to taste.

3 Meanwhile, cook the salmon fillets on a hot griddle pan or under a preheated hot grill for about 4 minutes on each side, or until just cooked through. Spoon the lentils on to serving plates, top with the salmon fillets and serve.

preparation time
15 minutes

cooking time
10–15 minutes

serves 2

nutritional values per serving
- 350 kcals
- 14 g fat
- 3 g saturated fat
- 7 g fibre
- Source of phytoestrogens

halibut with italian broad beans

200 g (7 oz) fresh or frozen broad beans
4 teaspoons olive oil
1 onion, chopped
4 rashers of smoked back bacon, chopped
2 courgettes, cubed
1 garlic clove, finely chopped
8 canned artichoke hearts in brine, drained and halved
handful of marjoram, chopped
handful of flat leaf parsley, chopped
2 halibut steaks, 175 g (6 oz) each
salt and freshly ground black pepper
lemon wedges, to garnish

1 Cook the broad beans in a saucepan of lightly salted boiling water for 4–5 minutes, or until just tender. Drain and plunge into ice-cold water to cool. Peel away and discard the outer shells and set the beans aside.

2 Heat 3 teaspoons of the oil in a nonstick frying pan, add the onion and bacon and cook for 5 minutes until softened. Add the courgettes and garlic and cook for a further 5 minutes, or until the courgettes are golden. Stir in the artichokes, herbs and beans and continue to cook for 1–2 minutes, or until heated through. Season to taste.

3 Place the halibut steaks on a lightly oiled baking sheet, brush with the remaining oil and season to taste. Place under a preheated hot grill and cook for 2–3 minutes on each side. Spoon the bean mixture on to 2 serving plates and arrange the fish on top. Serve immediately, garnished with lemon wedges. .

preparation time
10 minutes

cooking time
4–6 minutes

serves 2

nutritional values per serving
- 570 kcals
- 28 g fat
- 6 g saturated fat
- 13 g fibre
- Source of phytoestrogens

Cook's tip
Don't be seduced by large, smooth-skinned varieties of avocado – the small, knobbly Hass avocados have a creamier texture and better flavour.

griddled tuna with black-eyed bean and avocado salsa

1 large ripe avocado, peeled, stoned and diced
4 ripe plum tomatoes, quartered deseeded and diced
1 small red onion, finely chopped
300 g (10 oz) canned black-eyed beans, drained and rinsed
2 tablespoons chopped fresh coriander
finely grated rind and juice of 1 lime
2 fresh tuna steaks, about 150 g (5 oz) each
1 tablespoon olive oil
salt and freshly ground black pepper

1 To make the salsa, mix the avocado, tomatoes, onion and beans together in a large bowl. Stir in the coriander, lime rind and juice and seasoning to taste. Set aside.

2 Brush the tuna steaks with the oil. Place on a hot griddle pan and sear for 2–3 minutes on each side, or until cooked to your liking. Transfer the tuna to warmed serving plates and serve with the salsa

preparation time
20 minutes, plus chilling

cooking time
35 minutes

serves 2

nutritional values per serving
- 350 kcals
- 14 g fat
- 2 g saturated fat
- 2 g fibre
- Source of phytoestrogens

Cook's tip
Instead of frying the fishcakes, bake them in a preheated oven at 200°C (400°F), Gas Mark 6, for 20 minutes. Don't purée the potatoes in a food processor or they will be too sloppy.

smoked haddock fishcakes

150 g (5 oz) smoked haddock

250 g (8 oz) floury potatoes, such as Desirée or King Edward, cut into large chunks

2 tablespoons plain soya yogurt or cream

3 spring onions, finely chopped

plain flour, for dusting

1 egg, beaten

50 g (2 oz) fresh breadcrumbs, made from Miracle Bread (see page 132)

1 tablespoon vegetable oil

salt and freshly ground black pepper

To serve

lemon wedges

Tofu and Garlic Dip (see page 56)

1 Place the fish in a large, shallow pan and pour over just enough water to cover. Bring to the boil, then reduce the heat, cover and simmer for 8–10 minutes, or until tender. Flake the fish, discarding the skin and bones. Set aside.

2 Meanwhile, place the potatoes in a large saucepan of lightly salted water, bring to the boil and cook for 15–20 minutes, or until tender. Drain well, add the soya yogurt or cream and mash until smooth. Add the fish and spring onions, mix well and season to taste. Cover and chill for at least 30 minutes.

3 Turn the mixture out on to a lightly floured work surface and shape into 4 fishcakes. Carefully dip each fishcake into the beaten egg, then into the breadcrumbs, making sure they are evenly coated.

4 Heat half the oil in a large frying pan and cook 2 fishcakes over a high heat for 4 minutes on each side, or until the breadcrumbs are golden brown. Drain on kitchen paper, then transfer to a warm oven while you cook the remainder. Serve with lemon wedges and Tofu and Garlic Dip.

vegetarian
dishes

preparation time
15 minutes

cooking time
30 minutes

serves 2

nutritional values per serving
- 400 kcals
- 8 g fat
- 1 g saturated fat
- 13 g fibre
- Source of phytoestrogens

fragrant vegetable tagine

$1/2$ tablespoon olive oil
$1/2$ red onion, thinly sliced
1 garlic clove, crushed
pinch of ground cumin
1 teaspoon harissa (chilli paste)
50 g (2 oz) ready-to-eat dried apricots, roughly chopped
1 large carrot, thickly sliced
$1/2$ red pepper, cored, deseeded and roughly chopped
200 ml (7 fl oz) vegetable stock
300 g (10 oz) canned chickpeas, drained and rinsed
125 g (4 oz) cherry tomatoes, halved
1 tablespoon chopped fresh coriander
1 tablespoon chopped mint leaves
salt and freshly ground black pepper
couscous, to serve

Serve this lightly spiced Moroccan stew with couscous for an authentic meal.

1 Heat the oil in a large saucepan, add the onion and cook for 5 minutes, or until beginning to soften. Add the garlic, cumin and harissa and cook for a further 1 minute.

2 Add the apricots, carrot and red pepper to the pan and stir. Pour over the stock and bring to the boil. Season to taste. Reduce the heat, cover and simmer for 15 minutes.

3 Add the chickpeas and tomatoes and cook for a further 10 minutes, or until the vegetables are just tender. Stir in the coriander and mint and serve with couscous.

preparation time
15 minutes, plus marinating

cooking time
10–15 minutes

serves 2

nutritional values per serving
- 450 kcals
- 31 g fat
- 6 g saturated fat
- 6 g fibre
- Good source of phytoestrogens

tofu kebabs with indonesian salad

1 garlic clove, finely chopped
3 tablespoons dark soy sauce
1 teaspoon muscovado sugar
200 g (7 oz) firm tofu, drained and cut
into 2.5 cm (1 inch) cubes
125 g (4 oz) white cabbage, shredded
1 carrot, cut into thick matchsticks
175 g (6 oz) bean sprouts

Satay sauce
1 tablespoon vegetable oil
1 garlic clove, crushed
1 teaspoon chilli powder
75 g (3 oz) crunchy peanut butter
1 teaspoon muscovado sugar
150 ml (1/4 pint) water

1 Mix the garlic, soy sauce and sugar together in a shallow dish and toss with the tofu. Cover and leave to marinate for at least 1 hour. Soak 4 bamboo skewers in cold water for 30 minutes.

2 To make the sauce, heat the oil in a saucepan and add the garlic and chilli powder. Cook, stirring, for 1 minute. Add the peanut butter, sugar and measured water. Bring to a simmer and cook for 4–5 minutes, or until the sauce thickens.

3 Meanwhile, blanch all the vegetables in boiling water for 2–3 minutes so that they do not lose their crunchiness. Drain well.

4 Thread the tofu on to the soaked skewers. Cook under a preheated hot grill for 3–4 minutes on each side, or until browned. Serve the skewers on a mound of vegetables, with the satay sauce spooned over.

preparation time
10 minutes

cooking time
35 minutes

serves 2

nutritional values per serving
● 600 kcals
● 45 g fat
● 28 g saturated fat
● 2 g fibre
● Good source of phytoestrogens

Cook's tip
Thai green curry paste, available in most supermarkets, is a mild blend of spices including green chillies, lemon grass, coriander, garlic, kaffir lime leaves and lime juice.

thai-spiced tofu with spinach

1 tablespoon vegetable oil
200 g (7 oz) firm tofu, drained and cut into 2.5 cm (1 inch) cubes
1 onion, peeled and finely chopped
2 teaspoons Thai green curry paste
125 ml (4 fl oz) coconut cream
100 ml (3^1/$_2$ fl oz) vegetable stock
1 teaspoon Thai fish sauce (nam pla)
125 g (4 oz) fresh leaf spinach, roughly chopped
salt and freshly ground black pepper

Serve with Thai fragrant rice, or boiled brown rice.

1 Heat the oil in a large, heavy-based frying pan. Add the tofu and cook over a high heat for 2–3 minutes, or until golden. Add the onion and continue to cook for 2–3 minutes, or until softened. Stir in the curry paste and cook, stirring, for 1 minute.

2 Add the coconut cream, stock and Thai fish sauce and bring to the boil. Reduce the heat, cover and simmer over a low heat for 20 minutes.

3 Add the spinach in batches, stirring after each batch until it has wilted. Cook for a further 10 minutes. Season to taste before serving.

preparation time
15 minutes

cooking time
10 minutes

serves 2

nutritional values per serving
- 310 kcals
- 11 g fat
- 2 g saturated fat
- 1.5 g fibre
- Good source of phytoestrogens

Cook's tip
Tofu can be stored in the freezer for up to 3 months. If you can't find shiitake mushrooms use chestnut mushrooms instead.

tofu with pak choi and shiitake mushrooms

4 teaspoons vegetable oil
200 g (7 oz) firm tofu, drained and cut into 2.5 cm (1 inch) cubes
1 garlic clove, crushed
150 g (5 oz) shiitake mushrooms, roughly chopped
200 g (7 oz) pak choi, trimmed and roughly chopped
4 spring onions, finely sliced
2 tablespoons plum sauce
2 tablespoons light soy sauce
2 tablespoons water
125 g (4 oz) rice noodles

1 Heat half the oil in a wok or frying pan, add the tofu and cook for 2–3 minutes, stirring, or until it is golden brown. Remove with a slotted spoon and set aside.

2 Heat the remaining oil in the pan, add the garlic, mushrooms, pak choi and spring onions and cook for 2–3 minutes. Stir in the tofu, plum sauce, soy sauce and measured water and cook for a further 2 minutes, or until the sauce is hot.

3 Cook the noodles according to the packet instructions. Divide them between 2 bowls, spoon over the tofu mixture and serve immediately.

preparation time
20 minutes
cooking time
25 minutes

serves 2

nutritional values per serving
● 250 kcals
● 11 g fat
● 2 g saturated fat
● 7 g fibre
● Good source of phytoestrogens

roasted glazed tofu with stir-fried vegetables

200 g (7 oz) firm tofu
1 garlic clove, crushed
1 tablespoon hoisin sauce
1 tablespoon dark soy sauce
1 tablespoon sweet sherry vinegar
1 tablespoon sweet chilli sauce
2 teaspoons clear honey
2 teaspoons sesame oil
1 tablespoon sunflower oil
1 red onion, roughly chopped
1 carrot, cut into matchsticks
1 red pepper, thinly sliced
125 g (4 oz) broccoli florets
75 g (3 oz) mushrooms, quartered
4 spring onions, sliced
75 g (3 oz) sugar snap peas
150 g (5 oz) bean sprouts
2 tablespoons water
1 tablespoon toasted sesame seeds,
to garnish

Serve this delicious tofu dish with boiled brown rice for a satisfying main meal.

1 Drain the tofu, cut into 2.5 cm (1 inch) cubes and place in a shallow roasting tin. Mix the garlic, hoisin sauce, dark soy sauce, sherry vinegar, chilli sauce, honey and sesame oil together. Pour two-thirds of the mixture over the tofu and toss well to coat. Roast in a preheated oven at 220°C (425°F), Gas Mark 7, for 25 minutes, or until the tofu is deep golden brown and glazed, turning over halfway during cooking.

2 Meanwhile, heat the sunflower oil in a wok or large frying pan. Add the onion, carrot, red pepper, broccoli and mushrooms and stir-fry for 3 minutes. Add the spring onions, sugar snap peas and bean sprouts and stir-fry for a further 2 minutes.

3 Add the measured water to the remaining glaze and pour over the stir-fried vegetables. Cook for a further 2–3 minutes, or until the vegetables are just tender. Stir in the roasted tofu and serve topped with toasted sesame seeds.

preparation time
20 minutes,

cooking time
25 minutes

serves 6

nutritional values per serving
- 200 kcals
- 4 g fat
- 1 g saturated fat
- 8 g fibre
- Source of phytoestrogens

spicy bean burgers

1 tablespoon olive oil, plus extra for oiling
2 celery sticks, finely chopped
1 large red onion, finely chopped
1 large garlic clove, crushed
1 small red chilli, deseeded and finely chopped
2.5 cm (1 inch) piece of fresh root ginger, finely grated
875 g (1³/4 lb) canned mixed beans
1 teaspoon ground cumin
2 tablespoons chopped fresh coriander
plain flour, for dusting
1 egg, beaten
100 g (3¹/2 oz) fresh breadcrumbs, made with Miracle Bread (see page 132)
salt and freshly ground black pepper
Tzatziki
¹/2 cucumber
1 garlic clove, crushed
200 ml (7 fl oz) plain soya yogurt

1 To make the tzatziki, slice the cucumber in half lengthways and use a teaspoon to remove the seeds. Dice the flesh finely. Stir the cucumber and garlic into the soya yogurt and season lightly with salt and pepper.

2 Heat the oil in a nonstick frying pan, add the celery, onion, garlic, chilli and ginger and cook over a medium heat for 5 minutes, or until softened.

3 Drain the beans, then rinse well and drain again. Place in a blender or food processor and pulse until almost smooth. Add the onion mixture, cumin and coriander and season to taste. Mix together well. Turn the mixture out on to a floured work surface and shape into 6 burgers. Cover and chill for 30 minutes.

4 Dip the burgers into the beaten egg, then carefully coat in breadcrumbs. Place on an oiled baking sheet and cook in a preheated oven at 200°C (400°F), Gas Mark 6, for 20 minutes. Serve immediately with the tzatziki.

preparation time
15 minutes

cooking time
35–45 minutes

serves 2

nutritional values per serving
- 500 kcals
- 15 g fat
- 4 g saturated fat
- 8 g fibre
- Good source of phytoestrogens

spaghetti bolognese

1 tablespoon vegetable oil
1 onion, finely chopped
1 garlic clove, finely chopped
1 celery stick, finely chopped
1 carrot, finely chopped
75 g (3 oz) chestnut mushrooms, roughly chopped
1 tablespoon tomato purée
400 g (13 oz) canned chopped tomatoes
250 ml (8 fl oz) red wine or vegetable stock
pinch of dried mixed herbs
1 teaspoon yeast extract
150 g (5 oz) textured vegetable protein (TVP)
2 tablespoons chopped parsley
200 g (7 oz) wholewheat spaghetti
salt and freshly ground black pepper
freshly grated Parmesan, to serve

1 Heat the oil in a large, heavy-based saucepan. Add the onion, garlic, celery, carrot and mushrooms and fry for about 5 minutes, or until softened. Add the tomato purée and fry for a further 1 minute.

2 Add the tomatoes, wine or stock, mixed herbs, yeast extract and TVP. Bring to the boil, then reduce the heat, cover and simmer for 30–40 minutes, or until the TVP is tender. Stir in the parsley and season to taste.

3 Cook the spaghetti in a saucepan of lightly salted boiling water for 12 minutes, or according to the packet instructions. Drain well, then spoon on to serving plates. Top with the Bolognese mixture, sprinkle over a little Parmesan and serve.

preparation time
15 minutes

cooking time
10–12 minutes

serves 2

nutritional values per serving
- 523 kcals
- 31 g fat
- 5 g saturated fat
- 7 g fibre
- Source of phytoestrogens

penne with broad beans and feta cheese

200 g (7 oz) penne or other pasta shapes
200 g (7 oz) fresh or frozen broad beans
50 g (2 oz) sun blush tomatoes in oil, drained and roughly chopped
handful of mixed herbs, such as parsley, tarragon, chervil and chives, roughly chopped
50 g (2 oz) feta cheese, crumbled or roughly chopped
salt and freshly ground pepper

Dressing
2 tablespoons extra virgin olive oil
1 tablespoon sherry vinegar
1/2 teaspoon grain mustard

1 Cook the penne for 10–12 minutes in a saucepan of lightly salted boiling water, or according to the packet instructions. Refresh in cold water and drain well. Meanwhile, cook the broad beans in a separate saucepan of lightly salted boiling water for 4–5 minutes, or until just tender. Drain and plunge into ice-cold water to cool. Peel away and discard the outer shells.

2 Whisk the dressing ingredients together in a small bowl and season to taste with salt and pepper.

3 Place the beans in a serving dish and stir in the pasta, tomatoes and herbs. Toss with the dressing. Season with freshly ground black pepper and sprinkle over the feta.

preparation time
10 minutes

cooking time
25 minutes

serves 2

nutritional values per serving
- 441 kcals
- 13 g fat
- 1.5 g saturated fat
- 14 g fibre

Cook's tip
The easiest way to make Parmesan shavings is to use a vegetable peeler.

spaghetti puttanesca

1 tablespoon olive oil
1 garlic clove, crushed
pinch of chilli flakes
400 g (13 oz) canned chopped tomatoes
50 g (2 oz) pitted black olives, roughly chopped
1 tablespoon tomato purée
1 tablespoon capers
300 g (10 oz) canned flageolet beans, drained and rinsed
125 g (4 oz) wholewheat spaghetti
handful of basil leaves
salt and freshly ground black pepper
Parmesan shavings, to serve

1 Heat the oil in a nonstick frying pan. Add the garlic and chilli flakes and cook for 3–4 minutes. Add the tomatoes, olives, tomato purée, capers and beans. Reduce the heat and simmer for 20 minutes, or until the sauce is thick. Season to taste.

2 Meanwhile, cook the spaghetti for 10–12 minutes in a saucepan of lightly salted boiling water, or according to the packet instructions.

3 Drain the pasta and return to the pan. Sir in the sauce and the basil and toss well. Sprinkle over the Parmesan shavings and serve.

desserts

preparation time
10 minutes, plus freezing

cooking time
15 minutes

serves 4

nutritional values per serving
- 380 kcals
- 23 g fat
- 7 g saturated fat
- 0 g fibre

chocolate ice cream

500 ml (17 fl oz) vanilla-flavoured soya milk

250 ml (8 fl oz) soya cream

50 g (2 oz) caster sugar

3 large egg yolks

125 g (4 oz) plain chocolate, broken into pieces

1 Heat the soya milk and soya cream in a heavy-based saucepan until just below boiling point. Whisk the sugar and eggs yolks together in a large bowl until pale and thickened. Pour the hot liquid over the egg and sugar mixture, whisking all the time, then return the mixture to the pan. Place over a low heat and, stirring constantly, allow the mixture to thicken until it will just coat the back of a wooden spoon.

2 Remove from the heat and pour into a large, clean bowl, add the chocolate and stir well. Allow the mixture to cool, then pour it into an ice-cream machine and churn until the mixture becomes thick and frozen. If you don't have an ice-cream machine, transfer the mixture to a shallow, freezerproof container. Freeze for at least 1 hour, or until the mixture is just beginning to set around the edges. Remove the container from the freezer and beat the mixture until smooth, then return to the freezer. Freeze for a further 30 minutes, then beat again. Repeat the freezing and beating process several more times until completely frozen.

3 Allow the ice cream to soften in the refrigerator for 2 hours before serving. Any left over will keep for up to 4 weeks in the freezer.

preparation time
10 minutes, plus chilling

cooking time
5 minutes

serves 2–3

nutritional values per serving
- 465–310 kcals
- 24–16 g fat
- 12–8 g saturated fat
- 0 g fibre
- Good source of phytoestrogens

mocha pudding

75 g (3 oz) milk chocolate,
broken into pieces
250 g (9 oz) silken tofu
2 teaspoons instant coffee mixed
with 1 teaspoon boiling water
75 g (3 oz) soured cream
50 g (2 oz) sugar
1 teaspoon vanilla essence
1/2 teaspoon ground cinnamon

1 Place the chocolate in a heatproof bowl and stand over a saucepan of gently simmering water, making sure the bowl does not touch the water beneath. Allow the chocolate to melt, stirring from time to time.

2 Drain the tofu, place in a blender or food processor and process until smooth. Add the chocolate, coffee mixture, soured cream, sugar, vanilla essence and cinnamon and blend until creamy. Transfer to individual serving dishes. Chill thoroughly before serving.

preparation time
10 minutes, plus freezing

serves 2

nutritional values per serving
- 180 kcals
- 6 g fat
- 1g saturated fat
- 1 g fibre
- Source of phytoestrogens

banana and cardamom yogurt

1 large ripe banana, roughly chopped
300 ml (1/2 pint) plain soya yogurt
1 cardamom pod, seeds removed and crushed
2 teaspoons clear honey (optional)
raspberries, to serve

1 Place the banana, soya yogurt, cardamom seeds and honey, if using, in a blender or food processor and purée until smooth. Divide the mixture between 2 freezerproof bowls and transfer to the freezer for 1 hour.

2 Serve the yogurt with raspberries.

preparation time
15 minutes, plus freezing

cooking time
2 minutes

serves 2–3

nutritional values per serving
- 206–140 kcals
- 6–4 g fat
- 1–0.5 g saturated fat
- 1.5–1 g fibre
- Source of phytoestrogens

frozen strawberry yogurt

250 g (8 oz) strawberries, roughly
chopped, plus extra to serve
2 tablespoons purple grape juice
1 tablespoon crème de cassis
2 tablespoons icing sugar
300 ml (1/2 pint) soya yogurt

1 Place the chopped strawberries in a saucepan. Add the grape juice and warm gently, stirring occasionally, until the strawberries become soft and pulpy. Press the strawberries through a nylon sieve and collect their juice in a large bowl. Discard the seeds. Beat in the crème de cassis, icing sugar and soya yogurt.

2 Pour the mixture into an ice-cream machine and churn until the mixture becomes thick and frozen. If you don't have an ice-cream machine, transfer the mixture to a shallow, freezerproof container. Freeze for at least 1 hour, or until the mixture is just beginning to set around the edges. Remove the container from the freezer and beat the mixture until smooth, then return to the freezer. Freeze for a further 30 minutes, then beat again. Repeat the freezing and beating process several more times until completely frozen.

3 Store in the freezer for up to 2 weeks. Transfer from the freezer to the refrigerator 20 minutes before serving.

preparation time
time 5 minutes, plus soaking

cooking time
3 minutes

serves 2–3

nutritional values per serving
- 164–110 kcals
- 0 g fat
- 0 g saturated fat
- 5–3 g fibre

dried fruit compôte

150 g (5 oz) mixed ready-to-eat dried fruit, such as apricots, apples and prunes
300 ml (¹/₂ pint) orange or mango juice
200 ml (7 fl oz) boiling water
2 teaspoons arrowroot
250 g (8 oz) plain soya yogurt, to serve

1 Place the dried fruit in a large, heatproof bowl. Pour over the juice and the boiling water. Allow to cool, cover and leave overnight in the refrigerator.

2 Mix the arrowroot with enough cold water to make a smooth paste. Drain the liquid from the fruit and place in a small saucepan, stir in the arrowroot paste and bring to the boil. Cook for 1 minute, or until thickened, then pour over the compôte. Set aside and leave to cool. Serve with soya yogurt.

preparation time
10 minutes

cooking time
20 minutes

serves 2

nutritional values per serving
- 245 kcals
- 8 g fat
- 4 g saturated fat
- 2 g fibre
- Source of phytoestrogens

apple custard

1 large Bramley apple, peeled,
cored and sliced
2 tablespoons caster sugar
2 tablespoons water
1 heaped tablespoon custard powder
250 ml (8 fl oz) vanilla-flavoured
soya milk
125 ml (4 fl oz) Greek yogurt
toasted flaked almonds, to decorate

1 Place the apple slices, half the sugar and the measured water in a small saucepan, cover and cook over a low heat for 10 minutes, or until soft. Beat with a wooden spoon to make a thick purée.

2 Place the custard powder and remaining sugar in a heatproof bowl and mix to a smooth paste with a little of the soya milk. Bring the remainder of the milk almost to the boil in a saucepan, pour on to the custard powder and mix well. Return the mixture to the pan and bring to the boil, then reduce the heat and simmer for 1 minute, stirring constantly, until thick.

3 Allow the custard to cool, then stir in the puréed apple and Greek yogurt and mix well. Spoon into serving dishes and chill. Decorate with toasted flaked almonds before serving.

preparation time
5 minutes

cooking time
5 minutes

serves 2

nutritional values per serving
- 50 kcals
- 0 g fat
- 0 g saturated fat
- 2 g fibre

summer fruit compôte

250 g (8oz) mixed summer fruit, such
as raspberries, blueberries and
strawberries, thawed if frozen
finely grated rind and juice of
1 large orange
1 tablespoon redcurrant jelly
250 g (8 oz) plain soya yogurt, to serve

1 Place the fruit, orange rind and juice and redcurrant jelly in a large saucepan. Cover and cook gently for 5 minutes, or until the juices flow and the fruit is softened. Remove from the heat and set aside. Chill and serve with soya yogurt.

preparation time
10 minutes, plus chilling

cooking time
5 minutes

serves 2

nutritional values per serving
- 41 kcals
- 0 g fat
- 0 g saturated fat
- 2 g fibre

Cook's tip
If the remaining mixture has set before the final step, place it over a saucepan of gently simmering water until it becomes liquid again.

blueberry and elderflower jelly

3 tablespoons elderflower cordial
600 ml (1 pint) water
2 gelatine leaves
125 g (4 oz) blueberries

1 Mix the elderflower cordial with the measured water. Place 4 tablespoons of the mixture in a heatproof bowl, add the gelatine and leave to soak for 5 minutes. Place the bowl over a pan of simmering water and stir until it has dissolved. Stir the mixture into the remaining elderflower cordial mixture.

2 Divide the fruit between 2 large glasses, pour in enough of the liquid to just cover the fruit, then chill for about 30 minutes, or until just set.

3 Pour on the remaining liquid and chill for 3 hours, or until completely set.

preparation time
10 minutes

cooking time
25 minutes

serves 2

nutritional values per serving
- 328 kcals
- 14 g fat
- 5 g saturated fat
- 3 g fibre
- Good source of phytoestrogens

apricot risotto

200 g (7 oz) canned apricots in natural juice, drained
400 ml (14 fl oz) vanilla-flavoured soya milk
1 tablespoon caster sugar
15 g (^{1}/2 oz) butter
50 g (2 oz) arborio rice
50 g (2 oz) ready-to-eat dried apricots, roughly chopped
2 tablespoons toasted flaked almonds, to decorate

1 Place the canned apricots in a blender or food processor and purée until smooth. Place the soya milk and sugar in a saucepan and heat gently, stirring occasionally, until the milk reaches simmering point. Reduce the heat to very low and allow the milk to simmer.

2 Melt the butter in large saucepan, add the rice and cook, stirring, for 1–2 minutes. Add the dried apricots and cook for a further 1–2 minutes.

3 Add a ladleful of the warm milk and cook, stirring continuously, until the liquid is absorbed. Continue adding the milk in the same way until all the milk is used and the rice is tender – it will take about 20 minutes. Stir in the puréed apricots, then spoon into bowls and decorate with toasted flaked almonds.

preparation time
10 minutes, plus standing

cooking time
30 minutes

serves 4

nutritional values per serving
- 420 kcals
- 16 g fat
- 8 g saturated fat
- 3 g fibre
- Source of phytoestrogens

bread and butter pudding

5 thick slices of white bread
40 g (1^1/2 oz) butter
125 g (4 oz) sultanas or raisins
3 eggs, beaten
750 ml (1^1/4 pints) vanilla-flavoured
soya milk
50 g (2 oz) caster sugar
1 tablespoon demerara sugar, plus
extra for sprinkling
pinch of grated nutmeg

1 Remove the crusts from the bread, thinly spread with butter, then cut into triangles. Place half the bread in the bottom of a buttered 1.5 litre (2^1/2 pint) shallow, ovenproof dish. Sprinkle over the dried fruit and arrange the remaining bread on top, buttered-side uppermost.

2 Beat the eggs, soya milk and sugars together in a bowl. Strain the mixture, then pour over the bread. Allow to stand for 15 minutes.

3 Place the dish in a large roasting tin and pour enough hot water into the tin to come halfway up the sides of the dish. Sprinkle with the nutmeg and a little extra demerara sugar and cook in a preheated oven at 180°C (350°F), Gas Mark 4, for 30 minutes, or until set and the top is crisp and golden. Serve immediately.

Variation
For a pudding with a nuttier texture which is richer in phytoestrogens, use Miracle Bread (see page 132) instead of white bread.

baking

preparation time
15 minutes

cooking time
15–20 minutes

makes 6 muffins

nutritional values per muffin
- 210 kcals
- 6 g fat
- 1 g saturated fat
- 1 g fibre
- Source of phytoestrogens

Cook's tip
If you don't have any apricot jam, use a little warmed marmalade instead.

carrot and orange muffins

butter, for greasing
150 g (5 oz) self-raising flour
1/2 teaspoon baking powder
75 g (3 oz) caster sugar
finely grated rind and juice of 1 orange
125 g (4 oz) carrots, coarsely grated
100 ml (3 1/2 fl oz) soya milk
2 eggs, beaten
2 tablespoons sunflower oil
1 tablespoon apricot jam, warmed

1 Line 6 muffin tins with paper muffin cases or grease the tins well. Sift the flour and baking powder into a bowl and add the sugar, orange rind and grated carrot. Mix together and make a well in the centre. In a separate bowl, mix the soya milk, eggs, orange juice and oil together. Pour the liquid into the flour and stir until just blended.

2 Fill the muffin cases or tins two-thirds full with the mixture. Place in a preheated oven at 200°C (400°F), Gas Mark 6, for 15–20 minutes, or until a skewer inserted into the centre comes out clean. Transfer the muffins to a wire rack to cool.

3 Brush the tops of the muffins with a little warmed apricot jam and serve immediately.

preparation time
20 minutes, plus standing

cooking time
1¹/₄ hours

makes 2 loaves

nutritional values per slice
- 111 kcals
- 7 g fat
- 1 g saturated fat
- 2 g fibre
- Good source of phytoestrogens

fruit bread

75 g (3 oz) golden linseeds
75 g (3 oz) soya flour
125 g (4 oz) plain flour
125 g (4 oz) porridge oats
50 g (2 oz) sunflower seeds
50 g (2 oz) sesame seeds
50 g (2 oz) flaked almonds
200 g (7 oz) sultanas or ready-to-eat dried apricots
1 teaspoon ground cinnamon
750 ml (1¹/₄ pints) sweetened soya milk
To decorate
1 tablespoon apricot jam, warmed
toasted flaked almonds

1 Place the linseeds in a blender or a food processor and process for 30 seconds. Alternatively, grind them in a clean coffee grinder. Place all the dry ingredients in a large bowl and mix well. Pour over the soya milk, mix again and allow to stand for 30 minutes. If after 30 minutes the mixture seems too stiff, add a little more soya milk.

2 Line two 500 g (1 lb) loaf tins with greaseproof paper and spoon the mixture into the tins. Bake in a preheated oven at 190°C (375°F), Gas Mark 5, for about 1¹/₄ hours, or until a skewer inserted into the centre comes out clean.

3 Allow to cool in the tins for 5 minutes, then turn out on to a wire rack to cool completely. Brush with a little warmed apricot jam and decorate with toasted flaked almonds before serving.

preparation time
10 minutes, plus freezing

cooking time
15 minutes

makes about 20 crackers

nutritional values per cracker
- 80 kcals
- 5 g fat
- 2 g saturated fat
- 1 g fibre
- Source of phytoestrogens

Cook's tip
The crackers can be stored in an airtight container for up to 1 week.

linseed crackers

100 g (3^1/$_2$ oz) wholemeal flour
100 g (3^1/$_2$ oz) plain white flour, plus extra for dusting
^{1}/$_2$ teaspoon baking powder
^{1}/$_2$ teaspoon bicarbonate of soda
3 tablespoons golden linseeds
pinch of salt
50 g (2 oz) butter
3 tablespoons olive oil

1 Sift the flours, baking powder and bicarbonate of soda together into a bowl, adding any bran left in the sieve. Stir in the linseeds and the salt. Rub in the butter and oil, then add enough water to make a smooth dough (about 1 tablespoon should be enough).

2 Roll out the dough on a lightly floured work surface to about 5 mm (^{1}/$_4$ inch) thick. Cut out rounds with a 7 cm (3 inch) plain cutter. Transfer to a lightly greased baking sheet and bake in a preheated oven at 200°C (400°F), Gas Mark 6, for 15 minutes, or until golden brown. Remove from the oven and leave to stand for 1 minute before transferring to a wire rack to cool.

preparation time
20 minutes, plus proving

cooking time
30–35 minutes

makes 2 loaves

nutritional values per slice
- 110 kcals
- 4 g fat
- 0.2 g saturated fat
- 2 g fibre
- Good source of phytoestrogens

Cook's tip
To knead the dough, stretch it away from you with the heel of your hand, then gather it up towards you. It is ready when it will stretch without breaking.

miracle bread

300 g (10 oz) strong plain white flour, plus extra for dusting
350 g (11^1/$_2$ oz) strong plain wholemeal flour
50 g (2 oz) soya flour
2 teaspoons salt
2 teaspoons fast-action dried yeast
1 teaspoon caster sugar
2 tablespoons sesame seeds
2 tablespoons poppy seeds
2 tablespoons golden linseeds
2 tablespoons sunflower seeds
2 tablespoons pumpkin seeds
450 ml (3/4 pint) warm water
1 tablespoon flax seed oil
2 tablespoons malt extract
mixed seeds, for scattering

1 Mix the flours together in a large bowl. Stir in the remaining dry ingredients. Make a well in the centre and gradually add the warm water, oil and malt extract to form a soft dough. Turn out on to a lightly floured work surface and knead the dough for about 10 minutes, or until smooth and elastic. Return the dough to the bowl, cover with a clean, damp cloth and leave to rise in a warm place for at least 1^1/$_2$ hours, or until doubled in size.

2 Lightly oil two 1 kg (2 lb) loaf tins. Knead the dough again, knocking out the air, then divide in half. Shape the dough into 2 loaves and press into the prepared tins. Cover loosely and allow to rise for 30 minutes, or until the dough reaches the tops of the tins.

3 Brush each loaf with a little water and scatter over a few mixed seeds. Bake in a preheated oven at 220°C (425°F), Gas Mark 7, for 30–35 minutes, or until risen and golden brown. Leave in the tins for 10 minutes, then transfer to a wire rack to cool.

If you prefer to make rolls, divide the mixture into 24 equal portions and place on a lightly greased baking sheet. Bake for 15–20 minutes.

preparation time
10 minutes

cooking time
25–35 minutes

makes 9 bars

nutritional values per bar
- 250 kcals
- 15 g fat
- 7g saturated fat
- 3 g fibre
- Source of phytoestrogens

Cook's tip
Store the bars in an airtight container for up to 5 days.

banana and three-seed energy bars

100 g (3^1/$_2$ oz) unsalted butter
3 tablespoons golden syrup
150 g (5 oz) porridge oats
2 bananas, about 250 g (8 oz) in total
100 g (3^1/$_2$ oz) ready-to-eat dried prunes, roughly chopped
25 g (1 oz) pumpkin seeds
25 g (1 oz) sunflower seeds
25 g (1 oz) sesame seeds

1 Lightly grease an 18 cm (7 inch) square baking tin and line the base with nonstick baking paper. Melt the butter and syrup in a heavy-based saucepan until dissolved. Remove from the heat, add the remaining ingredients and mix well.

2 Spoon the mixture into the prepared tin, level the surface and bake in a preheated oven at 180°C (350°F), Gas Mark 4, for 20–30 minutes, or until golden brown. The mixture will still be very soft in the centre.

3 Leave to cool in the tin for 10 minutes, then cut into 9 squares. When cold, transfer to an airtight container. Don't try to remove the bars from the tin while they are still warm because they will break.

preparation time
15 minutes

cooking time
10–15 minutes

makes about 28 cookies

nutritional values per cookie
- 122 kcals
- 7 g fat
- 3 g saturated fat
- 0.5 g fibre

peanut butter and banana cookies

125 g (4 oz) butter, softened
150 g (5 oz) caster sugar
1 egg, beaten
1 teaspoon baking powder
125 g (4 oz) crunchy peanut butter
150 g (5 oz) plain white flour
100 g (3 1/2 oz) dried banana chunks, roughly chopped
28 unsalted peanuts

1 Place all the ingredients, except the banana chunks and peanuts, in a blender or food processor and process until well mixed. Stir in the banana chunks. Roll the dough into balls about the size of a walnut and place on lightly greased baking sheets, allowing enough space for the mixture to spread as it bakes. Using the palm of your hand, flatten the balls slightly.

2 Press a whole peanut into the middle of each cookie and bake in a preheated oven at 190°C (375°F), Gas Mark 5, for 10–15 minutes, or until just beginning to brown around the edges.

3 Allow to cool slightly. Using a palette knife, transfer to a wire rack to cool completely. Store in an airtight container for up to 5 days.

preparation time
20 minutes

cooking time
1 hour

makes 1 loaf

nutritional values per slice
- 220 kcals
- 12 g fat
- 2 g saturated fat
- 2 g fibre
- Source of phytoestrogens

banana and pumpkin bread

100 g (3^1/$_2$ oz) self-raising flour
75 g (3 oz) wholemeal flour
^{1}/$_2$ teaspoon bicarbonate of soda
1 teaspoon ground cinnamon
100 g (3^1/$_2$ oz) soft brown sugar
100 ml (3^1/$_2$ fl oz) sunflower oil
4 tablespoons plain soya yogurt
2 eggs, beaten
250 g (8 oz) peeled pumpkin flesh, coarsely grated
1 banana, mashed
50 g (2 oz) sultanas
50 g (2 oz) pecan nuts
2 tablespoons linseeds

1 Lightly grease and line the base of a 1 kg (2 lb) loaf tin with nonstick baking paper.

2 Sift the flours, bicarbonate of soda and cinnamon into a large bowl. Stir in the sugar. Place the oil, soya yogurt and eggs in a separate bowl and whisk to combine. Pour the liquid into the flour and beat with an electric whisk for 1 minute.

3 Stir in the pumpkin, banana, sultanas, nuts and linseeds and transfer the mixture to the prepared tin.

4 Bake in a preheated oven at 180°C (350°F), Gas Mark 4, for 1 hour, or until a skewer inserted into the centre comes out clean. Allow to cool in the tin for 5–10 minutes, then carefully transfer to a wire rack to cool completely.

preparation time
20 minutes

cooking time
30–40 minutes

makes 10 slices

nutritional values per slice
- 180 kcals
- 6g fat
- 3g saturated fat
- 1g fibre
- Source of phytoestrogens

Cook's tip
The gingerbread is best left to mature for 1–2 days before eating.

gingerbread

125 g (4 oz) plain flour
50 g (2 oz) soya flour
2 teaspoons ground ginger
1/2 teaspoon bicarbonate of soda
50 g (2 oz) sultanas
1 tablespoon preserved ginger in syrup, finely chopped
1 tablespoon linseeds
50 g (2 oz) butter
50 g (2 oz) brown sugar
50 g (2 oz) golden syrup
50 g (2 oz) treacle
3 tablespoons soya milk
1 egg

1 Grease and line a 15 x 23 cm (6 x 9 inch) shallow tin with greaseproof paper. Sift the flours, ground ginger and bicarbonate of soda together into a bowl. Add the sultanas, preserved ginger and linseeds.

2 Place the butter, sugar, syrup and treacle in a small saucepan and heat gently until melted. Add to the flour mixture together with the soya milk and the egg. Mix lightly.

3 Pour the mixture into the prepared tin. Bake in a preheated oven at 180°C (350°F), Gas Mark 4, for 30–40 minutes, or until a skewer inserted into the centre comes out clean. Allow to cool in the tin for 5 minutes, then turn out on to a wire rack to cool completely. Store in an air tight container for up to 1 week.

preparation time
15 minutes

cooking time
35–40 minutes

makes 10 slices

nutritional values per slice
- 136 kcals
- 2 g fat
- 2.5 g saturated fat
- 0.5 g fibre
- Source of phytoestrogens

cornbread

1 large egg
200 ml (7 fl oz) plain soya yogurt
25 g (1 oz) butter, melted
125 g (4 oz) fine cornmeal
50 g (2 oz) plain flour
1 tablespoon baking powder
1 teaspoon salt
pinch of cayenne pepper
1 large red chilli, deseeded and finely chopped
4 spring onions, finely sliced
125 g (4 oz) fresh or canned sweetcorn kernels
50 g (2 oz) freshly grated Parmesan

1 Lightly grease and line the base of an 18 cm (7 inch) square cake tin with nonstick baking paper. Whisk the egg in a bowl until frothy, then stir in the soya yogurt and melted butter.

2 Stir in the cornmeal, flour, baking powder, salt and cayenne pepper. Add the remaining ingredients and mix thoroughly.

3 Turn the mixture into the prepared tin and bake in a preheated oven at 180°C (350°F), Gas Mark 4, for 35–40 minutes, or until a skewer inserted into the centre comes out clean.

4 Allow to cool in the tin for 10 minutes, then turn out on to a wire rack. When completely cold, cut into squares..

preparation time
15 minutes

cooking time
35–40 minutes

serves 8

nutritional values per serving
- 400 kcals
- 32 g fat
- 13 g saturated fat
- 2 g fibre
- Source of phytoestrogens

lemon and seed cake

175 g (6 oz) butter
175 g (6 oz) caster sugar
2 large eggs, beaten
150 g (5 oz) ground almonds
75 g (3 oz) polenta or fine cornmeal
1/2 teaspoon baking powder
2 tablespoons linseeds
finely grated rind of 2 large lemons
2 tablespoons lemon juice
icing sugar, to dust
raspberries or blueberries, to serve
Lemon syrup
75 g (3 oz) caster sugar
finely grated rind and juice of 1 large lemon
2 tablespoons water

1 Line the base of an 18 cm (7 inch) springform cake tin with nonstick baking paper and lightly grease the sides. Cream the butter and sugar together in a large bowl until light and fluffy, then gradually beat in the eggs. Add the almonds, polenta or cornmeal, baking powder, linseeds, lemon rind and juice and mix well.

2 Spoon the mixture into the prepared tin and bake in a preheated oven at 180°C (350°F), Gas Mark 4, for 35–40 minutes, or until a skewer inserted into the centre comes out clean. Leave to cool in the tin.

3 To make the syrup, place all the ingredients in a small saucepan and heat until the sugar dissolves. Boil for 1 minute, then remove from the heat.

4 Remove the cake from the tin and transfer to a serving plate. Using a cocktail stick, prick the cake in several places. Drizzle over the syrup. Dust the cake with icing sugar and serve with fresh raspberries or blueberries.

index

Acknowledgements
Executive Editor Nicola Hill
Executive Art Editor
   Rozelle Bentheim
Editor Katy Denny
Designer Miranda Harvey
Picture Librarian Jennifer Veall
Assistant Production Controller
   Aileen O'Reilly
Photographer William Lingwood
Food Stylist Lucy McKelvie

Additional Photography:
Corbis UK Ltd/Rick Gomez 25 **Getty Images**/Frederic Lucano 21/Julie Toy 9 **Octopus Publishing Group Limited**/Frank Adam 12, 14 top, 18 detail 3/Colin Bowling; Organon Laboratories Ltd 11 top right; Schering Health Care Ltd 11 bottom left/Sandra Lane 17/Gary Latham 24/Peter Pugh-Cook 19 detail 1/William Reavell 14 bottom, 18 detail 2, 18 detail 5, 18 detail 6, 19 detail 5, 20 detail 4, 20 detail 5, 20 detail 6, 20 detail 7, 22/**Science Photo Library**/Sheila Terry 11 bottom right